ELEVEN

WWW.PHILLIPBRANDE.COM

To: Nicole the love of my life
and to Quinn and Aurora
the inspiration for Q&A

CONTENTS

Q&A
INTERVIEW

Q - I just finished reading your book and enjoyed it. You have a very interesting and different writing style. Though, it took me a moment to get use to it I found it to be very effective.

Phillip - I'm never really sure what to say when it comes to those types of statements but Thank You and I'm glad you enjoyed it. You are right it is written differently so I think there will be some people who love the way it is written and others that will hate it.

Q - Can you describe for us how it is written and how you developed that style?

Phillip - I'm not sure how the style developed completely. It is something that just happens while I'm writing and its sort of poetic in nature. There is a rhythm to it and once you find the rhythm in the writing it should create an experience in your mind and soul.

Q - But every section is not written in the same style,will what you just said hold all the way through the book?

Phillip - That is correct, different "sections" are written differently but that is the Art of it. Writing is not just putting words on paper its creating the most effective "voice" for the material you are writing about. When it comes to writing something that is based on a Bible passage it is a challenge to write into the text your experience with the living word of God and to do so in a way where that experience is felt as someone reads it. I'm not sure if I accomplished that task in this book or not, I'm waiting for the readers to let me know.

Q - This book is on Proverbs 11 which is odd to me that you would choose this one chapter to write a book about rather than the whole book of Proverbs. Why did you choose to write only on Proverbs 11?

Phillip - That's a good question and one that almost made me not publish this work. I agree it is odd to have a book written about one chapter in Proverbs and to choose chapter 11 as the source material is strange if not odd.

The church I pastor has read through the book of Proverbs a chapter a day every year in January. My blog would have a corresponding devotional to coincide with that reading. This is not a new idea other churches do this as well.

Last Spring (in 2014) I began to try to figure out a different way to go through Proverbs with the People at the church and came up with he idea to pick a chapter with 31 verses in it, we would then do a verse a day and challenge the people at the church to meditate and or memorize the verses as we went. So I begin to write the corresponding blog post just to see if it would work and found that there was plenty of information to write about.

As I researched and wrote on Proverbs 11 I began to play with the idea of putting what I was writing into book form. I have never written a book that I intended to publish until now. So that was how "Eleven" came to be.

Q - In this book you have a version of the Bible I have never heard of called… lets see… the PBP. Where did you find that version of the Bible?

P - Well, the PBP is the "Phillip Brande Paraphrase". It's not really a translation though sometimes it is directly from the Hebrew as best as I can translate but most of the time if not every time it is a combination of my studying of that verse combined with a translation of the Hebrew text. So, it's more of a paraphrase of those verses.

Q - In your opinion, how should people read this book?

Phillip - My suggestion would be to use it as a daily devotional and for people to really take time to meditate on the Proverb that is represented in each chapter. But however someone wants to read it is fine with me.

Q - Do you have any more books coming out soon?

Phillip - I have a few ideas for some but I want to see how this book does then pray about what to do next.

Q - Thanks for taking the time for me to interview you today

Phillip - No problem, anytime.

11:1

There are none among us…

at least if you love God…

who would want to do anything He despises.

Who would make Him want to repel us…

Doing things that would bring us under His judgment.

The Scriptures clearly tell us what some of those things are…

They are called abominations.

For example…

Idolatry, worshiping a false god instead of, or in addition, to worshiping God is an abomination – Deut. 7:25

Human sacrifice – When people get the notion that sacrificing their son or daughter to a false god by killing him or her is a good idea. Deut 12:31

Occult activity – (Which should go without saying). If you are participating in dark arts, witchcraft, Ouija boards, palm readings, having pentagrams as your favorite design, if you go to someone so you can talk to a dead relative, when you can't get enough of heavy metal that curses God, proclaims rebellion against Him and claims Satan as your leader-these are abominations to the God who created you. Why wouldn't it be? Deut 18:9-14

All abominations… to God

He hates these things

"Hates 'em"

In the same regard

There are none among us

at least if you love God…

who would want to miss out on being someone God delights in.

Who wouldn't want to make sure we were acting in ways that would call down the favor of God on us…

on our lives

Someone God looks at and says "they bring Me joy"

The Scripture is clear on the things God delights in

For example…

God is delighted when our number one desire is to seek the Lord and we make a commitment to follow Him – 2 Chronicles 15:15

God is pleased when we do His will regardless of how we feel – Ezra 10:11, Psalm 103:21

When we turn to Him in our time of need, putting our trust in Him to the point He becomes our refuge. Psalm 5:11-12

When our words and the thoughts of our heart are God-honoring – Psalm 19:14

When our spirit is humble not prideful – Psalm 51:17-18

He delights in those who listen to godly wisdom – Proverbs 8:32-35

Those whose goal is to do good to others - Proverbs 11:27

Those who tell the truth and do not lie even if it is not in their best interest to do so – Proverbs 12:22

Those who seek forgiveness from God and find relief by it - Proverbs 14:9

Those who pray, who talk to God on a continual basis - Proverbs 15:8

The Lord delights in those who marry correctly - Proverbs 18:22; and stick with the commitment they have made to each other. – Malachi 2:13-17

He delights in those who strive to live righteously so much so, He sent His Son to die on a cross and to rise again to make sure we would have the opportunity and power to do so.

No one…

if they love God…

would desire to live in any other way than a way that is pleasing in His sight.

And for anyone who desires that, Proverbs 11:1 causes us to stop a moment and ponder, for it is a verse that tells us something God delights in after informing us on an action He doesn't.

It's a verse about how you balance your scales and it's not in terms of balancing "right and wrong"

A false balance is an abomination to the Lord,
but a just weight is his delight – Proverbs 11.1 (ESV)

Back in the day when this was written most businesses were based off of how much something weighed. As a "store owner" you would have to purchase product to sell. The value of an item was based on how much it weighed so when you were purchasing an item to sell in your store you would weigh it and then buy it from your supplier. Then you would "stock your store" with the item and turn around and sell it to your customers and you would bring the scales back out again and adjust the value of the product so you could make a bit of profit for the time you spent working to get the product to them.

Basically it was like our wholesale value and resale value system

Which is no big deal; it's how businesses should run…

but just like now there were those who were dishonest about it. They would tip the scales in their favor. In fact, they would go as far as to have one scale they weighed the product they were buying from their supplier and then use a different scale to sell the product to their customers. The scales they used when they were purchasing items were intentionally set by them to weigh things a bit lighter than they really were so they would cheat the supplier out of the fair "warehouse" value. The scale that was used to sell items to their customers was; you guessed it, intentionally set to weigh heavier so they could sell the item for more than it was worth to the customer who did not have a clue they were being robbed.

This was giving people a "false balance" so that you could make more money unfairly

it was stealing

it was a dishonest business practice,

it was an abomination to the Lord… He hated it...

and He still does.

When someone intentionally deceives another person, someone they are making a business deal with, God is not pleased…

It's right up there next to burning your children to death

It's when you cheat the guy you are buying a product from by forcing him to sell to you low deceitfully, then you turn around and sell that product to a customer for a higher price than it is worth.

This is an abomination to the Lord.

But God delights in the business owner that does things correctly; the one that doesn't adjust his scales for his own benefit. The owner makes sure things weigh the same coming in as they do going out. He is not out to swindle someone, to steal from them, to sell something for more than it's worth. He does things honestly.

God delights in those types of business deals.

What is interesting in this verse; however, (at least to me) is not necessarily that God wants business owners to operate fairly, but the fact that the Lord is actively involved in the world of business and desires uprightness in business dealings.

This shows there is no difference to God between the secular and the sacred.

There is no church life and then our daily interactions.

There is not a "separation of church and business life" here on earth.

It is all together…

The secular is sacred

Because the sacred and secular are intertwined, "the secular" should always operate with a desire that is focused on honoring God in everything the business does, especially when it comes to "how" we are making our money.   When honoring God is the priority, things will always be sold at fair value to people who have earned their money to be able to buy them.

God delights in that.

So when you sell a car…..

when you sell something on eBay,

when you have that yard sale,

when you give a price to a neighbor for work he has asked you to do,

make sure you are not asking more than the "stuff" is worth.

Do things right and know that God will be pleased with your efforts.

God hates cheating in the marketplace;
He loves it when business is aboveboard. Proverbs 11.1 (MSG)

11:2

Pride

I've arrived.

Pride

My abilities, My accomplishments, My Wisdom trump all others.

Pride

Comes from a word that means "to boil" and was used to describe a person who was arrogant and insubordinate. They were "boiling over" with self importance. (Proverbs 11:2)

Pride

My abilities, My accomplishments, My triumphs rather than God's.

It is a push for personal acclaim. A belief that "I should be noticed because I am great and have the answers everyone needs."

Pride

"I'm the coolest thing in the room"

When people find themselves living this way they never receive the honor they think they deserve and the dishonor they do receive goes unseen for they are blinded by their…

Pride

But

for those that show up with a desire to learn, grow and contribute.

The ones that live their lives with awareness that God is at work and they are just serving Him by playing their part in His plan.

Those that know when and whom to submit to and when and how to stand for what is right.

Those that go about their day not even thinking that they are God's gift to the world because they have a personal relationship with that amazing Gift.

For those who realize their place before God…

You know the

Humble

They are the ones that live with honor not sought after and wisdom they are shocked they have. (Proverbs 11:2)

Jack had "had" enough.

The lady that was in his Sunday school class that was speaking was wrong. How could she say that about them…

about those Northerners

about those Catholics!

The more she spoke the higher his emotions rose. She needed to be stopped and he was the man to do it. After all He was RIGHT…

he always was.

In a show of extreme personal brilliance he spoke up and gave his CORRECT point of view. So amazing was his defense of his point of view no one in the class responded to him…

not even the teacher.

He won… shut her down.

There was no way she could recover from his brilliance on the subject.

It was a good thing he was there to set her straight.

But "his win was not a win to everyone else in the room" for they really thought he had gone a bit overboard in his defense of his position. He had been rude and disrespectful though he never realized he was being viewed that way. In fact for everyone in the room he lost a bit of respect in their eyes, but from his limited point of view he thought he had gained the very thing he had unknowingly lost.

To make sure the teacher knew he was right he approached her after the class under the guise of "I just wanted to make sure I didn't hurt your feelings but you needed to know what you were saying was incorrect, so you will not embarrass yourself again. After all I just wanted you to know the truth."

Even though he again thought he was on the high road and had gained respect for being right, his "high road" was currently experiencing a major landslide that was taking him further down into the abyss of dishonor.

The "rush of greatness" he was currently feeling was in reality the feeling of a free fall, and he was blinded to it.

That's what pride does. It blinds us to how things really are around us. It makes us think we are all that and a bag of BBQ potato chips when in reality it is pushing us over a cliff into a free fall of dishonor, blinding us to that fall...

until it's too late.

When pride comes, then comes disgrace,
but with the humble is wisdom. Proverbs 11:2 (ESV)

Jane was the epitome of nice and her family was well respected in the community. In fact their accomplishments were well known because everywhere Jane went she told people about all the great things her kids and husband had accomplished.

But little did she know that all around, her family really wasn't known for all those great things she thought they were known for. Their standing in the community was not what she thought it was. Instead, they were viewed as being a bit stuck on themselves and many believed they thought they were perfect.

So, at best, people tolerated them and liked them ok. But they were never impressed like she thought they should be.

A fact that she sensed but never acknowledged.

A fact that ate away at the fabric of every friendship she tried to establish and hindered the family's involvement in every organization they ever wanted to be a part of.

When the family was approached about problems with their children or relational issues among friends it never went well. After all, how could these people think these things about us? "We have values, we have great kids, and we are the Smith's! The Smith's are not known for these types of things!"

Her pride in her family and their achievements prevented her from listening to constructive criticism and stamped out any significant future opportunities for her family.

In seeking honor there was dishonor though they were unable to see it.

That is what pride does; it causes us to believe that others think we are really something, when in reality people are indifferent towards us.

When pride comes, then comes disgrace,
but with the humble is wisdom. Proverbs 11:2 (ESV)

Respect was what he always wanted to have. He overdid his job, spoke at every staff meeting and wore the finest clothes he could afford. He gave 110% of his effort to everything. But every year at the business Christmas party where employees were honored for their contribution to the company, his name never made that list. In fact as time went on he was invited less and less to the staff meetings and eventually not at all.

Unable to get over the hurt of it all, one day he spoke with a friend in the office about it. The friend told him the truth. "You're trying too hard, man. Stop trying to make a name for yourself… just relax and things will get better."

Upon hearing this news he became very angry with his friend. Not because he didn't think that what was said was true… he knew it was. He was angry because he had been unsuccessful in hiding his true motives.

"He wanted to be known as the best thing to hit that company ever."

That night he could not get to sleep at all, and finally in a weak state he confessed his sin of pride to the Lord and decided to change.

The next day, the first thing he did at the office was apologize to his friend. Then from that day forward he set out to do his job to honor the Lord and help the company any way he could.

Instead of aspiring for greatness, he focused on being useful and helpful to others.

Because of this, in the coming days he was promoted and honored for being one of the wisest people in the company at the end of the year staff party. And when he was honored he was thankful for the recognition and it encouraged his soul.

And such is the way of the humble… they find wisdom.

When pride comes, then comes disgrace,
but with the humble is wisdom. Proverbs 11:2 (ESV)

11:3

Integrity

good word

it is often thought of as something that a person is because of the values they hold to and keep.

And the Lord said to Satan, "Have you considered my servant Job, that there is none like him on the earth, a blameless and upright man, who fears God and turns away from evil? He still holds fast his integrity, although you incited me against him to destroy him without reason." Job 2:3

Integrity is often seen as something one possesses if they have lived a certain way. If someone has lived as they should live.

When it comes to God it is a quality that is attached to someone who has obeyed Him. Someone who has lived as God has desired for all of us to live.

You know… Someone who is "upright"

"Obedient to God"

But what if integrity is not only meant as a description of how we have lived…

in the past…

but is also meant as an action word to guide our future?

What if Integrity

the good word

was allowed to guide and control our movements….

our actions?

Wouldn't it guarantee that we would live as God wants us to live?

Yes it would…

and it would open doors for us, it would light our path from day to day and give us clarity for life's challenges.

It would be our guide.

What if Integrity

the good word

was not only a statement of how someone has lived but a guide that shows us how to live and not destroy ourselves.

YES

Integrity

the good word

is not only a description of the "upright" living of our past, it is also a guide for us today and in the future that keeps us on the right path and off the path of destruction.

"the integrity of the upright guides them but the crookedness of the treacherous destroys them" Proverbs 11:3

Treacherous

not a good word

It describes a person who can't be trusted but seems like they can be; a person that seems faithful but never intends to be faithful. A person who is very deceitful in all their relationships.

ALL their relationships…

their marriage – Ex – 21:8; Mal. 2:14 (broken faith with her) their friendships – Job 6:15

in all their personal dealings such as contracts or covenants. Judge 9:23 – they never seem to pay their bills.

in their disputes over matters legal or otherwise. They spin things, situations for their benefit Jer. 12:6

and they paint a wonderful picture of their relationship with God…

a picture that is not true. Jer 9:2

Treacherous people always have to twist and turn everything they do and say, so they can stay afloat. They twist things to avoid being taken down. They will say whatever is needed to be said, true or false, about anyone or anything in order to make themselves look good.

They are crooked with purpose

They are crooked and find they have success in being such

but the good times are not as good as they could have been

and the bad times are crushing and hard.

And even if they survive in the good for a certain amount of time…

it is only survival and they never thrive.

It's just temporary; you can only live treacherously so long before you destroy yourself.

It's sad…

When one is always deceiving, always doing whatever he/she wants when he/she wants to, treating people good or bad depending on his/her need for them. When someone is willing to do any twisted, crooked thing that is needed to make it to the top…

He/She will eventually wind up in a place never intended...

a place of destruction.

The treacherous life is a life wasted, for it ends in destruction.

"the integrity of the upright guides them but the crookedness of the treacherous destroys them" Proverbs 11:3

You and I have dealings with people every day and choices to make concerning our actions.

Will we let our crookedness make our decisions, bending and breaking God's moral standard as we go our way or will we allow our desire to be upright, to do the right thing according to His will, influence us instead?

Will we allow integrity

(the good word)

to be our guide?

11:4

Ya can't buy your way outta this one bro

Nope

Cannot

you might have the money

you might have had the prestige

you may have been the one that could influence things "in the room"

you may have been able to buy your way out of the traffic tickets, and all the other things you were caught doing wrong…

you may have thought you were "all that"

the most powerful

the one that was untouchable

and had the T-shirt to prove it.

And maybe that is true for now but it is totally worthless when it comes to God and His wrath

Ya can't buy your way out of that

but the one you made fun of

rejected for their weirdo belief system

the ones who were bigots because they believed in Jesus and the Bible

who you always tried to use your money against…

the ones that you strategized to get rid of because they were not "up to your standards" the ones you thought were stupid and non-thinkers

will be the ones that are delivered when you aren't

not because of their money

power

prestige

prominence

or their influence

but because they chose to live for God

and accepted his gift of righteousness

That's why they will be saved from death....

and their lives are prolonged.

Once upon a time there were three very powerful, wealthy and prominent members of a church. What they wanted to happen in that church happened. What they didn't want to happen didn't happen. Even if something slipped through and started to happen that they hadn't approved of they would step in and stop it. With resources and influence at their disposal they outlasted pastor after pastor always making sure their way was the only way anyone was to follow.

After all they were the Godliest people they knew of. Their business sense was awesome, their successes in their line of work unmatched and running the church their way was a breeze.

But in all their business wisdom, power, biblical knowledge and influence they missed one key thing...

Jesus

and because they missed Jesus they missed what righteousness and Godly living really is. Righteousness and life in Christ are not found in the money you have, the successes you achieve, the amount of influence you have nor in the size of your bank account balance. It's found in…

Jesus

Time after time God would send one of his servants to their church to get their attention. Time after time they would ignore "the preacher" "the pastor" because he was not as well educated or as successful as they were. "He should just preach" they thought and let them… the smart ones… run the church.

But in this they missed Jesus. They missed what God was intending to do. In dismissing these servants of God they were, in turn, dismissing God and their eternal life for their faith was in their abilities and not in what God had done for them.

Soon time passed and each man died, because that is the way of things. They found themselves standing before God, with no money, no successes, no influence and no power. They were in the presence of His wrath and could not buy their way out or change their course as they headed toward the unintended destination of the destruction of their own making. Oh how in the end, they wished they had handled themselves more submissively.

Once upon a time there lived 3 rich and wealthy men who hired 3 lowly men to do their bidding. Day after day the lowly men served their bosses while the bosses competed and competed for who would be the greatest.

Evil was the way of the 3 rich men. Over and over again they involved themselves in questionable practices and would buy their way out of any recompense. They bought judges, lawyers and whoever else they needed so they could accomplish their objectives. They never even felt the impact of the cost because of the enormity of their wealth.

Religion was for the weak.

Jesus was for the stupid.

Riches were what really determined reality.

Riches were the only thing in the world that could change the course of history and mold the future.

At least that is what they thought.

As time went by each one died and found themselves in a situation where they could not "buy out" the judge. Their riches were of no consequence in that day…

the day of God's wrath.

But the three lowly men were not there on that day and it wasn't because they had not passed, on for they had. They were in a different place. They were in the arms of God, not because they were rich or powerful during their short time on earth.

No.

They, at different moments in their life,

one when he was 9,

another when he was 25,

and the 3rd when he was 53,

made decisions to follow Jesus. He became their Savior and the molder to their way of life. No they didn't have riches. They had righteousness that was given to them by God; therefore, they were delivered from God's wrath.

a wrath which is often referred to as type of death.

"Riches do not profit in the day of wrath, but righteousness delivers from death."
Proverbs 11:4 ESV

11:5

Life is a funny thing. It seems like, from a human stand point, that in order to have life you must limit the amount of rules you live by. After all, rules, by nature choke the life and fun out of anything you would like to accomplish or do.

Rules are often seen as the downfall to achieving enjoyment in this life.

The problem is the lack of rules doesn't fair that well in the real world and the funny thing is if you run your life with your own set of rules life has a way of tripping you up to let you know that the rules (that are not made by you) are important for maintaining life and true enjoyment. Life has a way of bringing the very trouble you caused right back full circle to your own doorstep.

Now we all desire to have smooth sailing in this life. This is a task that seems impossible to achieve but maybe it isn't as impossible as we might think. We know; for instance, that if we decide not to… let's say "get drunk and then drive" we are more than likely not going to kill someone in another vehicle versus driving home while intoxicated. Or even if we leave "driving" out of the equation, we are more likely to say something hurtful or embarrassing while under the influence and will pay dearly for it later thus tripping over the very thing we thought was giving us life, fun and enjoyment.

but it's not just choosing to get drunk…

often times people think if they just tell a little bit of gossip (information, of course) about someone else it will not bring any harm to anyone and it will help their cause. But gossip has a bit of a sting to it because it always seems to come back to haunt the gossiper at some level often taking another form when it does.

When people give others the cold shoulder they often come to a place later in life (sometimes 10 years or more) where they find they now need that connection with the individual they treated wrongly to accomplish a task and find themselves tripping over the very wickedness they caused that person years before.

It seems that in life people eventually stumble over the very thing, the very sin, the very wicked act they have committed against another person. People often make their own lives bumpy by the wicked choices they make whether they realize it or not. If a person lives as they want without regard for the "rules" God has given, that person never makes it to a life that has any semblance of smoothness to it. In fact they are constantly planting for themselves land-mines to step on or rocks to trip over on their future path. Things that would have never been part of their future if they had just chosen to live correctly.

"the wicked will" *always* "fall by his own wickedness."

Living that way makes life complicated.

~~Isn't life complicated~~ enough on its own without us making it more complicated by making sinful choices? Each choice we make, ~~good or bad, is either a choice to make our~~ life less complicated (when we do the right thing and stick with it) or more complicated (when we choose to live wickedly). The truth is choices that are right (according to God's Word) shine a bright light (that only righteousness can produce) onto our path, smoothing out most of the rough places life throws at us.

However, choices that are made that are sinful make a path rougher and darker, turning life into a complicated mess.

Choosing the wrong thing

the wrong way

the wrong action.

will always make things worse rather than better (even though for a time it will seem good).

But, to live a life that desires to do things right by following God and His rules even when we do not understand why He tells us to do things certain ways, is a life that becomes blameless. No one can point a finger at something in our lives that is truly wrong with what we have done. They can make up things, they can say all kinds of stuff about us but it will not be anything we will stumble over because we didn't do those things we have been accused of. We are able to continue to walk smoothly, stepping over the rocks that are being thrown onto our path, because the guiding light of the righteousness of God helps us navigate smoothly around them and even helps us dodge stones when they are thrown.

They however- the ones who are making up things about us — will not be so lucky. It is just a matter of time before the wickedness they have conjured up will become their own downfall.

It's not that when we live our lives the way God intends for us to that we no longer have conflicts…

No, we will have conflicts.

We will just have less of them and when they come we will be able to navigate through them in the best (smoothest) way possible. Conflicts are easier when we know we have been living for God and haven't done anything wrong. When we know for certain the conflict is not God judging us or is a result of our wickenedness.

It is important to note that "blameless" in this verse does not mean perfection; instead it means we have by God's grace avoided staining our soul by choosing to live unrighteous. We have chosen to live for Jesus as best as we can. It is this type of life that will not fail nor cause us to trip and is the life we all need to strive to have and live by.

11:6

Your desires drive you to do what you do.

Yes, whatever you do or go after in this life will always be driven by the desires that live in the deep places of your soul. Those desires only come in two forms….

good and bad.

Greed is a desire that is never classified as good. It is never deemed as a good motivation to do or achieve anything. Greed is all about me, what I want, what I can get and it produces sinful fruit. Jealously, covetousness, hatred, dishonesty, and a disregard for others are just a few of the sins it creates. Greed will do anything, break any rule, and get as dirty as is needed to accomplish the thing or item it is after.

These types of people…

Those that are motivated by greed…

by lust…

are considered to be…

Treacherous

Not safe

Not good

Not upright

They lay trap after trap. Always trying to get what they want by gaining the upper hand on the people that are around them. They seemingly have victory after victory. They gain; they dominate and are rude when they do it. They look down on those who can't help them achieve their goals financially or otherwise and they use everyone else. What they do not realize, what has never entered into the deep portions of their minds is with every victory, with every greedy, selfish gain that is accomplished; they are baiting a trap that will be used for their own capture…

and they will not escape it when it is sprung.

They will be caught by the very greed they used to capture the things they lusted after.

"... the treacherous will be caught by their own greed" Proverbs 11:6 (NASB)

"… the treacherous are taken captive by their lust." Proverbs 11:6 (ESV)

If we allow ourselves to be motivated by greed, (by lust) it will not end well for us.

There will be no deliverance, no one to set us free us from our trap, no one to save us from the destructive end we have set in motion.

There is only capture ahead for those who are motivated by greed.

But…

a desire to be righteous

a motivation to live right

is always classified as good and filled with deliverance, never capture. It's filled with freedom and not restriction.

Upright living is the result of a strong desire to live for God, His word and for that word to penetrate us, mold us and shape our lives. It's when we act on God-given direction and become upright in all our dealings and interactions.

It's when God himself is pleased because He knows our motivation is for Him and to please Him in all that we do.

When we live like that…

motivated by righteousness…

the things that we have done that "come home to roost", when our actions finally catch up with us…

we will find we have been delivered from the self inflicted heartache that those who have lived treacherously find themselves captured by. Because sometimes that is deliverance…

And if we find ourselves experiencing the adverse effects of someone else's bad choices in life, we will even be delivered from those. We will not be captured by them, for sometimes deliverance is from circumstances you did not create but just have to endure for a season.

Yes, living righteously does not produce the absence of adverse circumstances just the deliverance from them and the freedom of knowing you didn't create them with the desires of your heart.

The righteousness of the upright will deliver them, But the treacherous will be caught by their own greed. Proverbs 11:6 (ESV)

Deliverance is the lifestyle of all those who are motivated by righteousness, while capture is the lifestyle of all those who allow themselves to be motivated by greed. (Proverbs 11:6 – PBP)

Remember, your desires either drive you to be captured or to be delivered.

The choice is yours.

11:7

There are two different types of expectations in this world…

expectations that will perish

and those that will not.

Everyone has expectations, some of those expectations are tied to this world and others are tied to the spirit realm, their connection is with the Kingdom of God. People that choose to live this life with expectations that are only tied to this world will find, at the moment of death, every expectation they spent their life pursuing or accomplishing will perish with them.

That is sad…

Recently I ran across a YouTube video of a comedian that spoke about the rise of Atheist Mega Churches in America. Yes, as unbelievable as it sounds there are Atheist Mega Churches grounded in the belief that this life is all there is. If you see it you can go after it. If you are the weak link you will not achieve it and find death instead, for only the strong survive. There is no expectation of an afterlife or any type of god or spiritual existence. The only things that are real are grounded in this physical world that you see.

"What would people sing in an Atheist mega church?" Tim Hawkins asked. "Maybe it would be…

No one loves the little children, all the children of the world

or

Shout to the void all the earth let us sing, power and majesty, praise to nothing"

The Bible defines anyone that rejects the existence of God and the spiritual realm as wicked.

Wicked

But make no mistake, wicked people still have expectations in this life. Expectations of wealth, popularity, nice cars, nice houses, and great parties. The expectation to have influence over the shaping of organizations or businesses. Expectations of being able to provide for their children, having successful marriages, finding true love, being respected, or having the ability to invent something new for the world. Expectations of restaurants and of having enjoyment on vacations or with the performance of their favorite sports team(s). Expectations of having money in the bank and the security that financial stability brings them in this life.

They do not expect death though death is unavoidable. Death is something they cannot cheat or avoid. When death comes, all the expectations they carried and pursued in this life perish with them. The reality is, in a matter of a generation, the expectations they lived for will be forgotten as if they never existed.

Whatever they strive for

whatever they decide to do, whether in their eyes is "good" or "evil"…

whatever security they build up

whatever power they obtain in this life

whatever position of prominence they acquire

perishes with them.

It's a "vanity of vanities."

Such is the way of things that are tied to this world.

"When a wicked man dies, his expectation will perish, And the hope of strong men perishes." Proverbs 11:7 (ESV)

There are two different types of hopes in this world

hopes that will perish

and those that will not.

Everyone has hopes and dreams. Some are tied to this world and others are tied to the spirit realm and have their connection to the Kingdom of God. Those that choose to live this life with hopes that are only tied to this world will find at the moment of death, every hope they have desired, no matter how strong of a person they were, will perish with them.

The hope of love, of greatness, of respect, of power. The hope of a good legacy that will last, the hope of enjoyment and good health. The hope of happy times and advancement. The hope of a good family and the love of others. The hope for peace in the world and financial stability.

Strong men will position themselves with the hope that they are in the right place at the right time, so they can achieve their expectations and realize their hopes. The hope to defeat an enemy, to find a cure for cancer, to have the next big motion picture or record. The hope to win a battle or national sports title. The hope to go to Mars or live on a moon colony. The hope to end world poverty and famine.

These are all hopes tied to this world and can never be hopes that are sure to come to pass. They may or may not happen depending on how the world turns. If they do happen, the hope that is achieved only lasts for a brief season and soon will perish with the ones who hoped them into existence.

Such is the way of this world and the way of this life for all those who place all their hopes and expectations in what they see around them…

those that are wicked because they have no expectation or hope in God.

"When the wicked die, that's it— the story's over, the end of hope." Proverbs 11:7 (MSG)

Living wickedly is a sad way to live.

11:8

There was a prophet of sorts, a wise man if you will, in the Old Testament named Daniel. Daniel was a good man, a righteous man, a wise man and he had made some enemies.

Not on purpose.

Not because he chose not to like them and therefore they didn't like him.

No it was nothing of that sort. Instead it was because they were jealous of his position. Specifically his friendship and influence with the king. An influence they wish they possessed. They were so jealous and hated him so much. Because of this jealousy, they decided they needed to get rid of him. So they thought and thought of ways they could achieve their goal.

Day by day they watched to see if Daniel did anything wrong that would be considered treason or illegal. They watched his goings and comings to see if he mixed with the wrong people or if he had some bad habit no one knew about that they could exploit. But they could not find anything to pin on him so they could point their fingers at him and accuse him of some treacherous deed in front of the King. A deed that would have him excommunicated from their presence and taken permanently out of their lives. The problem is they couldn't find anything.

There was no dirt to dig up on Daniel.

So they went back to the drawing board and came up with a plan to make a law against something that Daniel believed in. Because if you can't find anything wrong with someone the next step is to attack his religious practices. The source of his righteousness.

They knew that in order to get a righteous person to break the law you must write a law into existence that states they can no longer do a religious practice that they were in a "religious" habit of doing. A religious practice that they could make a law against. Something that would not even put their faith to the test. Something you knew they would do anyway even if it was outlawed.

Like…

a law that says you can no longer pray to Jesus.

So with much consideration and persuasion they convinced the king to sign a law into existence that stated everyone had to pray only to him… the king.

No exceptions.

If someone was caught praying to anyone else besides the king the punishment was death. But not just any death. You would be thrown into a Lions Den to become their food for that evening.

This is what evil people do. They use politics to cause trouble for the people they are mad at, upset with, or jealous of. They have secret meetings to scheme and bring people to their side. Then they set their schemes into motion so they can get rid of the people they are not willing to submit to, that they are jealous of, so they can have the power their pride says they deserve. If it hurts or takes the life of the one they hate…

so be it.

But something happened that the enemies of Daniel did not expect in their wildest dreams. After "partying" through the night Daniel was thrown into the Lions Den, they woke up the next morning only to find their scheme had not worked. It had actually backfired with repercussions for them and their families.

Why didn't it work?

Was it because Daniel decided not to pray to God and pray instead to the human King?

No

Was it because the Lions were not hungry that evening or they just didn't like Jewish cuisine?

No

Was it because Daniel figured out a way to escape out of the den, a way no one else knew about?

No

Was it because he held onto a rock suspended above the lions all night until the King came the next morning to pull him out?

No

Instead, the scheme didn't work because God delivered Daniel

God delivered him

and then God made sure those wicked individuals and their families were never able to harm his servant again. That's why the enemies of Daniel wound up taking Daniel's place in the Lions Den along with their spouses and their children.

And the king commanded, and those men who had maliciously accused Daniel were brought and cast into the den of lions—they, their children, and their wives. And before they reached the bottom of the den, the lions overpowered them and broke all their bones in pieces. Daniel 6:24

The righteous is delivered from trouble and the wicked walks into it instead. Proverbs 11:8 (ESV)

Wicked people are wicked

and

Righteous people are righteous

Because of this there will be conflict between these two groups and sometimes war. The wicked; however, are the ones who always strike and scheme to rid themselves of the righteous. They scheme and contemplate ways they can get rid of or gain power over the one who is living for God. They stir up trouble, for their own benefit.

But what they forget

or neglect to acknowledge

is God

And when trouble is brought to the doorstep of one of his servants by people with wicked hearts, he is not only going to deliver his servants from that trouble, he is going to bring the trouble back on the wicked ones who started the mess in the first place.

(Another example is in the book of Esther, Mordecai is saved from the gallows and the schemer Haman takes his place.)

Who are the people in your life that are trying their best to cause you harm? The ones that are trying to cause you trouble? Who schemes against you to rid themselves of your existence? All for power and control!

Who are they?

Have no fear. Even when things seem to be going wrong, the days become dark and you suffer for living for God. You will be delivered. I do not know how, I do not know when. But God will set things right and the wicked will reap the trouble they intended for you.

That's the way of things

"The righteous person is rescued from trouble, and it falls on the wicked instead."
Proverbs 11:8 (NIV)

11:9

They will say it…

and say it again

and again.

Anything and everything they can to destroy someone

Slander is their way

The Rumor mill is their equipment

making someone look bad is their goal

they are godless.

"With his mouth the godless man would destroy his neighbor..." Proverbs 11:9a (ESV)

The godless are the ones that pull you aside to tell you how they have been wronged by your boss, or by another co-worker. In church, it's the person that has you over and the topic of conversation revolves around someone they do not care for that much, someone they present as being wronged by. They of course are "the innocent good ones" and you leave your visit with them wondering how "that person" in your church could treat these "godly people" so wrongly. It is in that moment that you couldn't be further from having the truth of the matter. You have bought into a lie and deemed someone godly that is anything but godly. The discussion you allowed yourself to have with them should have been your first clue that you were not in the presence of someone that was righteous. They are using you and they know it's just a matter of time before you spread their lie to someone else thus aiding them in their destructive agenda.

But time reveals the truth of things, it always does. So before you start spreading lies that are intended to destroy someone to others, you may want to wait and see what the real truth is. That is better than being played as an instrument of destruction and will save you some embarrassment when the truth finally does come out.

But that embarrassment is not as bad as the feeling that you get when you find out you are on the receiving end of someone's slander. When you see godless people smear your name to others. When you feel and notice the changes in those relationships. You are hurt because you know those people have believed a lie about you and have turned their backs on you. You feel helpless because you fear God and are committed to living correctly. You can't have a conversation with those who have been swayed. To have a conversation like that would be sin. The godless ones and their lies about you seem to be winning. They are moving in for the kill and your hands are tied. So, you do the only thing you can do…

you pray for deliverance

This is a hard spot to be in…

I have been there

and you, more than likely, have had a similar experience.

So what do you do?

You wait, because in time the truth brings with it the knowledge that others have lied and you have been delivered from their attempt to destroy you.

"With his mouth the godless man would destroy his neighbor, but by knowledge the righteous are delivered." Proverbs 11:9 (ESV)

I have also been there

when the tables were turned by the truth coming to light.

And what a moment it was.

So…

that person who keeps saying things about you that are not true and are hurtful. Who has hit the airwaves with things about you and has seemingly turned people against you. Be patient, for one day the truth will be known. They will be seen for who they are and you will be seen for who you are.

Knowledge of truth always wins the day; it just might take some time.

on the other hand…

If you are the person who is slandering and spreading lies about someone know this…

today you may be on top and people are signing on to your corrupt and hateful agenda but you will not win.

You will not win

A righteous person cannot be destroyed

time will pass

and with time comes truth

and with truth comes knowledge

and you will be seen for who you are and what you are trying to do

and the one you have tried to destroy with your senseless words…

will be lifted up.

They will be delivered.

"With their words, the godless destroy their friends, but knowledge will rescue the righteous." Proverbs 11:9 (NLT)

11:1O

"When it goes well with the righteous, the city rejoices, and when the wicked perish there are shouts of gladness." Proverbs 11:10 (ESV)

It's always good when the good guy wins

Movies demonstrate it

Books show it

Life demands it.

But it is not just "the good guy winning" that is meant here. It's when the righteous prosper; when they are the ones giving leadership and direction to a society. When things are going well for the righteous and they are leading, oppression is reduced if not wiped out. Justice becomes something people can trust in again because there is a clear set of values to judge things by. No one wonders if justice will be done because the righteous do not base their decisions on what they feel like on a given day or on whoever grabbed their ear first (with their version of the story). Instead, they listen and decide based on a set of morals they did not write or come up with themselves. When they are in control the living environment for everyone is better.

There is peace when the righteous prosper.

There is security. People live in safety.

There is economic growth

Fear is nonexistent

If riots happen the righteous speak out against the senseless violence and take steps to put a stop to protect businesses that are being looted and burned by the protesters. When the wicked are met with resistance from those who stand for true justice, it always calms situations down and never stirs them up. Wicked people can't get away with harming innocent people when righteous people are in control.

Because righteous people make decisions that are good for all people. Their decisions are not based on race or economic status but on what is right and what is wrong. Righteous people know there are right actions and wrong actions regardless of who you are or what you stand for. All people become important when the righteous prosper, not just one select group of people, special interest group or otherwise.

When the righteous are in power it allows all people to succeed honestly. When they are in control, when the righteous prosper, everyone has a sense of self worth and stability. Regardless of their economic status or race.

People are happy

You can see this in a church, a business, a family, or even the government. If someone that is wicked is over the business the employees suffer. The same is true of Churches and governments. You see this especially when leadership changes. In a matter of weeks if the transition was from selfish wicked people to righteous ones the organization goes from an oppressive state to a refreshing one. From a feeling of "I just can't please them" to "I want to do my best for them".

This is a fact of life.

"When the righteous prosper, the city rejoices; when the wicked perish, there are shouts of joy." Proverbs 11:10 (NIV)

It goes something like this…

For too long the people were under the control and rule of an evil and corrupt leader. His decisions were unjust, his policies crippling and his intentions all self focused. Bent on power and maintaining it he would remove any obstacle to accomplish his goal of dominion, regardless of the consequences.

People lost their lives, the economy crumbled and the people lost their jobs. Sometimes the innocent were caught in the line of fire. The days were dark and it wasn't because the sun had quit shining.

Then, out of the blue, came one man who decided to stand up against the tyranny. Actions and situations ensued; battles were fought until finally the good one defeated the evil and freed the people from the destructive environment that had been created.

Then the city, everyone who was left, rejoiced in the victory of the one who had the courage to stand and fight and see it through to the end.

But there was not only rejoicing in the one who had saved them. There were also shouts of gladness because the wicked and their ways had perished.

No longer did men hide themselves - Proverbs 28:12

The days of groaning were over - Proverbs 29:2

for the wicked had perished and righteousness had won the day.

Sounds like a fairy tale huh?

So what does it look like in life?

It's the end of WWII when Hitler was finally defeated and the world rejoiced (even though some of us were not alive during this we have seen footage of that celebration)

It was the day the Boston bombers were dealt with.

It is the day the Israelites walked out of Egypt freed from slavery by the mighty hand of God.

It was the day you could sit anywhere on a bus and drink from any water fountain regardless of the color of your skin.

It was the day the bully in your school got what was coming to him.

It was the day the presidency changed to someone who was more competent in that role.

It was the moment that the person who had done "anything" they could to gain a promotion, paid for all the deception they had stirred up to get there. In the end their lack of righteous integrity destroyed them.

It was the day you walked away from your job because you could not work under that type of corruption anymore and since then you have witnessed the demise of that organization.

It was the day you were let go from your job but it forced the company to deal with the individual who caused all the issues…

and you received the news they had been dealt with…

and you were glad.

Not because of revenge

but because now there is freedom for the people left behind…

and your leaving seems all the more worth it.

Because when the wicked perish…

it's ok to rejoice and be glad.

This verse should motivate our prayers. We first need to ask God to help/enable us to be people who live righteously and make decisions based on His. We need to repent of the wickedness we feel at times in our hearts and ask God to deal with us concerning it. Then and only then can we start lifting up our communities, our churches, and the leadership of our local, state and federal governments, asking that God would strengthen the righteous leaders that are currently serving in those positions and raise up more God fearing righteous people to replace all the wicked unrighteous ones. Our prayer is that God will enable the righteous to prosper in all they do and for Him to remove wicked people. Yes, as the old preacher once said, "from the court house to the white house to your house" our prayers concerning this need to be lifted up.

and when God answers….

there will be much rejoicing and dancing in the streets.

I'm looking forward to that day!

"When it goes well for good people, the whole town cheers; when it goes badly for bad people, the town celebrates." Proverbs 11:10 (MSG)

11:11

How do you feel when....

you're around someone who talks positively about their family? Not in a bragging, my children are "all that" sort of way. In a positive manner, they speak positively about their children and their spouse and even if they criticize something concerning them it still comes across as positive and real.

Do you know anyone like that?

How do they make you feel?

How do you feel when...

you're around someone that talks positively about their job and the company they work for? They speak highly of their boss and the team of people they work with. When there is an issue and they speak of it, that too comes across as positive. Even in the issues they speak of, they never cast a bad light on the company they work for. It's not that they are blind to the weaknesses of the company they just recognize there's always stuff to work on and they do not sweat it or have a bad attitude concerning those things. Even when they talk about them it is not in a derogatory way and you never get the sense that they are upset. They believe in their company and support it. There's no doubt about that.

Do you know anyone like that?

How do they make you feel?

How do you feel when...

you are around someone who talks positively about their church and their pastor? They speak highly of the things that are happening at their church but not in a self righteous irritating sort of way. They are real about things without having an edge. When they speak about anything that is a weakness that their church has, it is always with an understanding they are actively being part of the solution to solve it. You never get the sense they are upset or even worried about if things are done their way or not. They feel good about their church. There's no doubt of that.

Do you know anyone like that?

How do they make you feel?

I bet it makes you feel good or at least thankful. You leave those people not feeling burdened or upset about anybody or anything. You leave feeling blessed and there's a reason for that.

The people you were just around are righteous followers of God and bring blessings on everything they are involved with or are part of. They use their words to build people and places up. They are always giving life and solution to circumstances that would wind up being worse if they did otherwise…

and you can bet that they are praying for their family, the company they have a job with and their church on a regular – daily basis. It's hard to talk bad about something that is always taken to God in prayer. These people are a blessing to be around and bless others with their words and actions. They are upright in all they do and say.

"Through the blessing of the upright a city is exalted…" Proverbs 11:11

How do you feel when…

you are around someone who is trashing their spouse? Their spouse never does anything right. Story after story is told about things that their spouse has done that is stupid or inconsiderate. There are complaints about football, 31 parties, giggling women in the house, hunting season, cooking, and cleaning. Everything is bad. They are always left taking care of the children while their spouse gets to go out and have a good time somewhere else. They speak of their sex life (which makes you uncomfortable… maybe) and joke about that. Soon they move on to the children. First up is the child who is just like the spouse they have trashed earlier in the conversation. From the way they talk they have the worse kids ever. If the spouse or the children show up in the room and interrupt this conversation they make them look bad in front of you. When the conversation ends it leaves you with the feeling that they think "if it were not for them" the place would fall apart because of all the incompetence and stupidity that exists in their household.

Do you know anybody like that?

How do they make you feel?

How do you feel when…

you're around someone that is constantly trashing their job? Their boss is stupid and unreasonable. They are never treated right. The hours are too long. The work environment is strenuous and difficult. They can't believe they were asked to do some task that they consider beneath them or is not part of their job description. They cannot wait to get out of there and find another job. In fact they say they are looking for another job and maybe they are and maybe they aren't. Things are always bad at work…. always.

Do you know anybody like that?

How do they make you feel?

How do you feel when…

You're around someone that is talking negatively about their church? The pastor didn't treat them right, and the rest of the leadership team is worthless. They don't care for the music. The services are too long. The church has no vision. The sermons are watered down. They do not like some of the people in the church and elaborate on why. The church is unfriendly. No one ever talks to them anymore. They tell you story after story about how this bad thing happened and how this event didn't go well and how this person doesn't have a clue what they are doing. They speak of conflicts that are occurring. To them nothing good is happening at their church.

Do you know anybody like that?

How do they make you feel?

I am willing to bet they make you feel bad and hopeless. You leave their presence with grief and concern. You leave thinking that their family, the company they work for or their church is in a mess and you wish you could do something about it. You may even leave upset at some of the people they have spoken about.

There's a reason why you feel that way.

They are wicked and they are using their mouth for destructive purposes.

"Through the blessing of the upright a city is exalted, but by the mouth of the wicked it is destroyed." Proverbs 11:11 (NIV)

These types of people never pray for their family, the company they work for or their church. Instead they spend time with anyone who will listen while their mouths vomit words of destruction. In short, their attitude stinks.

Words have power and the words that people use not only reveal the condition of their heart (Luke 6:45) but words can also either bless or destroy.

Which do you do with your mouth?

We need to be people that use words that are a blessing to others. It's not that we sweep bad things under the rug and ignore reality in order to be positive. Instead we make sure our attitudes towards our families, friends, the company we work for and our church doesn't stink. We make sure we are not speaking about things out of hurt or pride and when we do speak it's out of love. Love that doesn't ignore wrongs but approaches them with the absence of a crummy attitude. Love that intends to handle and bless. Words that build up, fix and help others succeed; not get mad and destroy.

Will you be a blessing to those around you by living upright?

Or will you allow your words to destroy those around you by choosing to submit to the wickedness that is in your heart?

It's up to you.

"When upright people bless their families, their employer and their church with their words it makes a positive difference not only in those places but also in their communities. When wicked people talk down and criticize their families, their employer and their church it tears down and destroys not only those places but destroys their community as well." Proverbs 11:11 (PBP)

11:12

Neighbors are important

all of them

Yes, even the ones…

you know…

that are well…

"that way"

that are so easy to talk about or get upset at. The way they live (to you) makes it hard not to fall into the trap of saying…

"you'll never believe what my neighbor did yesterday….."

"My neighbor is so stupid…."

or

they seem to make it hard for you not to be upset at them. You get so upset that you find yourself wanting to go over to their house to give them a piece of your mind and that's just what you do.

"Whoever belittles/ derides (NIV)/ despises (NASB) his neighbor lacks sense…" Proverbs 11:12 (ESV)

Just the other day I was reading in the newspaper about a dispute between two neighbors. One neighbor had gotten so mad at the other neighbor that he decided to line his property with "not so nice" signs with words I shouldn't type here, addressing "in sign form" the issues they were fighting over.

Crazy

In another neighborhood (in America) a neighbor staged a one man picket line in front of his neighbor's house protesting the dispute they were having between each other. He looked absolutely ridiculous carrying his sign back and forth on the road in front of his neighbor's house.

Ridiculous

Another person in another neighborhood took her dog to her neighbor's house and allowed it to take a dump in the neighbor's yard. Then she proceeded to put a small sign up beside it that said "clean up your dog's mess when he poops in someone else's yard." (and it was IN ALL CAPS)

WOW

"Whoever belittles his neighbor lacks sense…" Proverbs 11:12a (ESV)

"Whoever uses vocalized negative expressions against their neighbor lacks sense…" (PBP)

There are times when our neighbors will do things that we do not understand, that will irritate us to no end. Everyone has a neighbor (or two) in his community that just isn't like everyone else. Some are cranky while others just need to be medicated (and they have never explored that option). But there are reasons why those neighbors are the way they are and the irritation you have towards them shows that you probably have more of a problem than they do. This may be especially true if you act out on those feelings - talking about them behind their backs or lashing out at them.

You think your neighbor lacks sense because of how he lives; but you prove you lack sense when you belittle him to his face or behind his back to others. Each word you speak against him proves that you "lack sense" even more so than he does.

Ouch… right?

"but a man of understanding remains silent." Proverbs 11:12b (ESV)

"but a man who refrains from speaking negative expressions against his neighbor is a man that understands the value of maintaining relationships." (PBP)

Here is what he "understands".

Neighbors are important.

Neighbors are important and it is unwise to say whatever it is that is on our mind concerning them. It causes damage… to us and them.

Neighbors are important. It is best to have peace with your neighbor and do what it takes to have peace and not stir up strife with them.

Neighbors are important and maintaining a good relationship with them is valuable. Rash comments or speaking unwisely causes you to lose a valuable connection with them.

Neighbors are important. Yes, there are neighbors that you should keep your distance from. There are Neighbors that should never be close to you. But, this fact does not mean that you can treat them bad or talk about them in a negative way.

You never know when you might need their help.

Neighbors are human and just like everyone else, they make mistakes. You never help someone by spreading what they have done to other people. You never help someone by yelling at them and getting upset. To stay silent keeps the door open for them to correct their lifestyle and keeps you from lying about them. It keeps a door open for them to seek you out for help in the future concerning their issues because you refrained from dragging them through the mud at the moment you were emotionally charged. It conveys the message that you are safe and a friend that is there to help and serve them instead of being their enemy.

Rash, belittling comments have a tendency to find their way back to the individual(s) they were directed at. We all know how this feels and what it does to us and our feelings toward the person who made the comments. The feeling of betrayal and shock that comes from those words damages our relationships with those "neighbors" from that point on.   The exact same thing happens when we say something that belittles someone else. It eventually gets backs to them and the damage is often irreparable.

Rash, belittling comments that we make about someone else, reveals how wimpy and unrighteous we really are. It is senseless to tell someone else about an issue you have with another person; it never solves the problem and makes it worse. When we allow ourselves to say something about someone that is not in the room that we would not say if that person were present reveals we are too cowardly to handle our grievances in the right fashion…

with just that person.

It proves that cultivating healthy relationships is not as important as maintaining our level of pride.

A man of understanding "understands" these things…

so he is silent

thus, he is careful when, if or how he speaks to the person concerning the issue that is on his heart.

"*Whoever uses vocalized negative expressions against his neighbor lacks sense; but a man who refrains from speaking negative expressions against his neighbor is a man that understands the value of maintaining relationships.*" Proverbs 11:12 (PBP)

11:13

"*…Slandering…*" (ESV)

"*He who goes about as a Talebearer…*"(KJV)

"A gossip betrays a confidence…" (NIV)

"*A gossip goes around telling secrets…*" (NLT)

all are different ways these translations of Proverbs 11:13 translate the Hebrew word רָכִיל (rakil – "raw-keel"). This word is only used six times in the Old Testament. "Rakil" in context here refers to someone who maliciously uses privileged, confidential information to his advantage.

We all have moments where sensitive information has to be shared. Sometimes it is with our spouse or within our immediate family unit. Other times it's with our best friends where we can vent a little bit and then they bring us back from our moment of insanity. Sometimes it's at work and information within a work group has to be shared to prevent a problem or handle one correctly. It's when you go to a counselor and share things that are going on with you that you do not want anyone else to know. It's in these moments we talk about information that would be damaging for us if what was said was to get out. Not that it was bad information but information that would be easily misunderstood. We are all faced with having to share sensitive information from time to time.

The danger we are all afraid of is the moment you find out there are individuals in the room that begin to use that private information for their own advantage. These types of people love controversy and use sensitive information to stir up trouble, especially if it hurts someone they want to get even with. They understand the power of information and the power of the tongue. They use both with evil purpose though they maliciously cover up their intent by coming across as "doing what is best" for the individual or group.

These types of people are untrustworthy and hurt the organization and get a kick out of the drama they have stirred up. They do not care if others are damaged by the information they share and may not even be aware of the damage they are causing.

It's almost like they are addicted to talebearing.

Sue revealed her feelings she was having for another man who wasn't her husband to one of her closest friends. From that conversation she realized that she needed to defeat the temptation by telling her husband about it. After she told him she never thought about "the other guy" in that way again.

But then the betrayal came

Her friend told a church member about it. That church member was in charge of recommending people to positions in the church. That person told a friend, who told another friend, who told another, and the story that was being told had little truth to it, for it had been expanded with every share. This broken confidence not only prevented Sue from having ministry opportunities but caused her family to leave the church. Her friend; however, was able to stay and take her place in the position that would have been Sue's otherwise.

So not only was Sue's family damaged, the church was as well.

We need to be on the lookout for these types of people and search for people who we can trust.

Whoever goes about slandering reveals secrets, but he who is trustworthy in spirit keeps a thing covered. Proverbs 11:13(ESV)

The phrase "he who is trustworthy in spirit" can literally be translated "the faithful of spirit". People who keep a lid on things; that do not gossip are a rare find. You can find a gossip anywhere. They are a "dime a dozen". But people who understand the importance of concealing private conversations, who are trustworthy and loyal in spirit, that are not out for themselves and their personal rise to power, that are humble and keep things to themselves for the good of all, are hard to find.

You never even catch them "slightly" referring to something that was spoken about in confidence.

They conceal those conversations…

they cover them up

they "keep a lid on it"

Therefore, your well being is always safe with this neighbor.

It is these types of people you should look for and make your closest friends.

There is something; however; more important for us to do than just look out for people who can't keep their mouths shut or for those whom we can trust and confide in. You and I need make sure that we are individuals people can trust and confide in. That you and I are "faithful in spirit". We need to be a place of safety, where information can be shared without threat of exposure.

Is that you now or do you need to change?

Have you shared something you shouldn't have?

Let's live our lives in ways where people can trust us and not for our own sakes.

"He who goes about using inside information to cause problems and for personal advancement should never be trusted, but he who is faithful in spirit can be confided in for they will keep information quiet and never use it for their own purposes." (PBP)
Proverbs 11:13

11:14

"Where there is no guidance, a people falls, but in an abundance of counselors there is safety." Proverbs 11:14 (ESV)

The word that is used here for guidance is a rare word in Scripture. It is a word that refers to steering or directing a ship by pulling ropes according to orders.

It's tacking according to how you are told to tack.

This was important to people who sailed back when Proverbs was written (and even now). This was especially important if you entered into a storm.

Imagine for a moment entering a storm on a ship without an experienced captain and a group of people who loved to be on a boat but knew very little about sailing. How do you think that would turn out?

Right… not very well at all.

When a ship was forced to enter a storm it became extremely important to have a capable captain and for the crew to listen his commands. If those commands were ignored it would jeopardize your life and all the lives of the people on board that vessel. Chances are, if you did not listen, no one would survive. A good captain knows the best way to get through a storm is to head directly into it. It is impossible to out run the storm. To survive, the ship must remain on course in the midst of the storm. To stay on course, tacking becomes very important. Sails must be adjusted and turned at the right moments. If you were one of the ones helping tack during a storm it would be all you could do to adjust, hold onto the ropes and hear the commands from the captain as they came to you. A "tacker" cannot guide the ship and tack at the same time. They can't see where they are going and tack effectively at the same time. This is especially the case when everyone on board is literally fighting for their lives. If there is no one to guide them…

they will perish.

That's why you need a captain. A captain can keep in tune with the storm because he is not trying to hold ropes tight nor is he working to make sure water doesn't flood the ship. His job is to keep track of exactly where the ship needs to go and do what is needed to get her there. For everyone else on the ship it is extremely important to listen to his directions. If he repeats the directions over and over sailors cannot allow the repetitiveness to cause them irritation. Instead they listen and accept them willingly, knowing their lives depend on his every word. Success in getting through a storm only comes from wise guidance...

the ship perishes without it.

Recently I was at a basketball game where both teams had good players. One team was coached well and the other team had a coach that really didn't understand the game. If both teams would have had good coaches, the game would have been close and frankly I'm not sure who would have won. But, because that was not the case, the well-coached team beat the other team by a 30 point spread. That's the power of a group of talented people having a good leader guide them. Guidance leads to victory.

"If a group of people have no guidance they will fail, they will lose and come into ruin

but if a group of people have an abundance of counselors

they will succeed." Proverbs 11:4 (PBP)

Duke is not my favorite basketball team. I do not hate Duke, but I do not pull for them either. What intrigues me about that team is not the players but the coach, Mike Krzyzewski. He is the main reason that school has had a successful basketball program year after year. I have seen Duke beat teams that have triple the talent that Duke had because of the wisdom Coach K brings to the table. A Wisdom that the players choose to listen to. A lot of basketball teams have an amazing line up but fail to win because of the lack of guidance available to them or because the players aren't humble enough to listen to the coach and do what he asks of them. Duke has winning season after winning season and it's not just because they have great players... it's because they have an outstanding coach.

They have guidance so they win...

That is the way it is in life.

Marriages that listen to wise counsel succeed. Spouses, who pick and choose people that are in agreement with their take on how the marriage is going, and should go, always fail.

Consequently, marriages that "try to make it on their own" do so at their own peril, but marriages that look for wisdom and guidance succeed.

Business partnerships, which seldom look for guidance outside of their company, never thrive or survive.

Communities that elect mayors and city council members that lack wisdom and also lack leadership skills will find that at the end of their term the community is in worse shape than when they elected them.

Churches that lack leadership waste away and never accomplish anything significant for God and His kingdom. When the church is filled with leadership in name only, leadership that never leads or gives guidance, the church diminishes.

From families, to communities, to church life or business life, if there are no leaders, if there aren't people stepping up to the plate to guide and help people move to a better day, failure occurs and people perish.

Lives are wasted

Resources are wasted

Nothing positive occurs.

Failure is the course when people have little to no instruction.

No one gets through a storm alive on their own

But if there is guidance, and that guidance is listened to, it leads to safety and success.

"but in an abundance of counselors there is safety." Proverbs 11:14b (ESV)

It's not just whether there are leaders around, if there are counselors around or people willing to give guidance. It's whether you and I look for those people, to make them part of our lives, to help us make good decisions along life's way.

Abundance means that we have listened to several people and their take on a given issue and we are making our decisions based on wise instruction that we have sought after and received. An individual that does this or a group of people that seeks after this, winds up succeeding.

They ensure their safety.

It's not just listening to a bunch of people sharing their "way of doing things." Sometimes there are more chiefs than there are Indians and no one gets anywhere. Everyone is confused and there is chaos. That's not what it is speaking of here.

It's speaking of us seeking wisdom from more than one person and then thinking, deliberating, contemplating what to do, and then making a decision based on the counsel we have received. To reject counsel and not listen to anyone is to fail.

It's the coach that studies the plays and ways of Mike Krzyzewski (Coach K) and applies what is applicable to the team he is coaching.

It's the couple that reads, watches and listens to other couples that have been married a while to find out how they made it or dealt with a certain issue and takes that information, thinks through what they could do or change to better their marriage.

It's the leaders of the community that look at other communities to figure out ways to be better leaders.

It's church leadership that looks outside its walls for wisdom on how to deal with issues and ministry.

It's when people decide to quit being self made and admit they do not have all the answers, opening the door for them to hear and listen to others so they can make good decisions.

It's when leaders lead.

It's when leaders guide

It's when coaches coach

and they are always looking for ways to lead better, guide more effectively and improve on their coaching skills.

When there are people looking for wise guidance from counselors and leaders dedicated to providing it; that communities, families, businesses and churches do not fail. They succeed and make it out of storms safely.

They succeed.

"Without good direction, people lose their way; the more wise counsel you follow, the better your chances." Proverbs 11:14 (MSG)

11:15

You know that good friend of yours

that wants you to co-sign for their loan

it's better if you don't do it.

for everyone involved…

You know that acquaintance of yours who wants you to be the surety for a debt they are about to undertake…

don't shake on it

don't do it

it will be better for you and everyone involved.

"If you promise to pay a stranger's debt, you will regret it. You are better off if you don't get involved." Proverbs 11:15(GNT)

It is a scary thing to put your financial stability into someone else's hands. It is a very rare occasion where doing something like this works out for the good. Wisdom is not being so quick to agree to be a surety for someone and in the RARE case where we do help someone in this way we should hate every minute of it.

Putting your financial stability into the hands of someone else and his choices is a scary thing to do.

I have a friend of mine that owns a car dealership. It is a small car dealership but he has nice cars partly because he cleans them up and makes them look as "new" as he possibly can…

It is amazing how he can transform the look of a vehicle.

His problem is not the quality of cars he sells or the diligence by which he works…

his problem is he allows people (strangers, acquaintances and friends) to take out loans with him (not a bank). He sets up the pay schedule and the loan terms. He takes a huge risk when he does this. It's like co-signing for a loan, and if they do not pay him he is left with financial loss.

Time and time again when people do not pay their monthly payment (which happens a lot) he is left in a predicament and it hinders the growth of his business. It paralyzes his ability to buy new vehicles because his money is tied up with friends and acquaintances that are not good at paying their bills. When they fall behind on their payments the business falls behind and he struggles to make ends meet at home. (There is a reason why people's credit prevents them from borrowing money.)

If he would just learn not to be the surety for other loans and; instead, get a bank in the area to handle the loans, he would no longer be stuck with the negative effects of late or nonexistent payments. It is not a good thing to place your financial stability into the hands of other people.

Sure, you can always "repo the vehicles" and resale them, but repossession is quite the process and often times (more than not) the person not making the payments isn't taking care of the car they have purchased. On the rare occasion he gets a car back, it is worth less than when he sold it. Add to that the cost of the repossession process and it equals a loss of revenue that is hard to overcome.

It is not a good idea to do business this way.

"Whoever puts up security for a stranger suffers harm..." Proverbs 11:15a

I have other friends who were missionaries to another country. Because they were gone from the country (USA) doing mission work for so long their good credit score was non-existent when they returned to the States. When they went to buy a car they could not get a loan because of their lack of "a credit score" and just between me and you… generally, (and unfortunately) pastors and missionaries are not people you should lend money too. Unless they have a good record with you, or are family, you should never co-sign a loan for them.

But in reality (and unfortunately) "regular" people are also not people to which you should lend money or co-sign a loan. We tend to forget that missionaries and pastors have the same struggles as most people. This is why you need to be careful with all people and not co-sign or loan money to them without much thought and consideration. Even then it is better not to do it.

In my friend's case; however, it was one of those rare moments where it was ok to help out. Though the situation was one that neither my friend nor his parents wanted to be in, his father co-signed the loan for his son and the car was bought. A payment was never missed and it built their credit back up to where it needed to be. Everything turned out the way it was supposed to.

".... but he who hates striking a pledge is secure." Proverbs 11:15b (ESV)

Even when it is someone you know that you are trying to help, though you might be "glad to do it," you should still be reserved enough to not be "all that glad" to do it. Wisdom does not enter into one of these agreements lightly. In fact there should be much resistance before accepting the responsibility of securing a pledge for another. But, even when you find yourself being the surety for someone else's loan this next statement is still true…

it is safer not to co-sign for anyone… ever.

Regardless of how you feel about him or her.

"There's danger in putting up security for a stranger's debt; it's safer not to guarantee another person's debt." Proverbs 11:15 (ESV)

11:16

"A gracious woman gets honor, and violent men get riches." Proverbs 11:16 (ESV)

From the first read of this Proverb it seems that women are being elevated and men are being slammed on. There are several reasons for this: First, our culture in general puts a negative spin on being a man (they are hardly ever presented as being good) and elevates the value of women. So we are programmed culturally to be ok with the man being the one with the problem and not the woman. For example, we have yet to see a Christian movie where the wife apologizes for something she has done; it seems to always be the guys that have to work on things, "get better" or change.

(Ok… yes that is a pet peeve… now on to something else.)

Second, up until this point in chapter 11 of Proverbs we have had contrast after contrast of evil and good; which sets us up to think in those terms. What we must keep in mind is Proverbs is a collection of individual, short, wise sayings and when we interpret Proverbs the immediate context doesn't always determine what is meant by a given verse.

Third, this is the only place in Proverbs where we find men and women "being contrasted." That fact alone should make us stop and investigate a bit further concerning what this Proverb is saying. Something is odd about that fact and it could be that this Proverb is not contrasting the two sexes in a negative way.

There are a few things about this verse that we need to note. For instance, it contains 3 sets of words that parallel each other,

women and men

gracious and violent

honor and riches.

At first glance, it seems this verse is a contrast of good and evil, and most translations lean that way. But that type of contrast doesn't work for several reasons. First, we know that not all women are gracious and not all men are violent. (Please don't tell the women I said that.) Second, the verb "attain" is used twice, once for the woman and then for the man and is used in a neutral sort of way. This fact alone brings us to the realization that neither the woman nor man is meant to be seen in a bad light and the honor and riches each attains is not a negative or sinful accomplishment in any way. Which brings us some questions, then why the use of gracious and violent? What is he trying to say to us by using those two words? They do not seem to fit the current pattern, could it be that one of them should be translated differently?

The answer the last question is yes…

and the word that needs to be translated differently is violent/ruthless.

Now, before you go throwing your translation away, what you need to know is 99% of the time the word that is used here for violent/ruthless is translated other places in the Bible as either… you guessed it…violent or ruthless and brings with it bad connotations. However, this is one of the few places in the Bible that the translation for the Hebrew word וְעָרִיצִים (wə-ʿā-rî-ṣîm,) should be translated in a more positive way. In this case, it should be translated "strong" instead of "ruthless." The King James Version puts it this way…

"A gracious woman retaineth honour: and strong men retaineth riches." Proverbs 11:16

This changes things.

We all go through life with our sights set on different things that we would like to attain. Some of those things are physical items of monetary value: cars, houses, boats, gold, land and diamonds to name a few. While, other times we go after the attainment of some sort of status or position like CEO, DR., or MRS. Nothing is wrong with pursuing these things. We all (men and women alike) should have things we have set our sights on that we would like to have or accomplish.

It is the way God designed us to be so we can succeed in this life.

There are right ways to gain the things we desire and wrong ways to go about achieving them. Men and women are designed by God to acquire those things in different ways. Women who go about attaining what they are after the right way do so graciously. It's the Proverbs 31 woman, who by the way is anything but wimpy. There is something about a woman that determines in her mind to go after the good things in this life, who accomplishes them correctly, that brings honor not only to her and her achievements, but also to her husband and her family. Here the Bible affirms the value of a gracious woman…

she is worthy of honor.

In other places Proverbs describes women who are anything but gracious. They go about attaining things in a sleazy, deceptive, evil sort of way. In the process of attaining those things they destroy every life they touch, including their own. There is no honor in what they do or what they accomplish. It's all destructive. But here in this passage the value of a gracious lady is exalted above the worthless ones.

They are honored.

Men; however, acquire things in a different way than women do. Men aren't exactly gracious in how they go about things. In fact, when a man expresses graciousness it always has an edge to it; just like when a woman expresses strength it always has a touch of graciousness to it. A man's edginess comes from the rough strength of heart that is divinely placed into him. Some men fight this "rough strength" because they are convinced by society they need to get rid of it because it is bad. But a man can never rid himself of those rough edges.

Rough isn't always bad.

Men acquire things by strength; the strength of their hands, the strength of their backs, their resilience, and their strength of mind. Men have a mind that is more logical and less gracious.   Here the acquiring of riches is not meant to be seen in a negative light.
 Instead, just like the statement about women attaining things correctly, this is also a statement of how a man attains riches correctly. He does that with the strength of his hands and the sweat of his brow. It's a good thing to earn riches by honest work.

In other places Proverbs warns us of being the type of man who goes about achieving his goals in evil ways. This always leads to destruction and judgment. Evil men hurt people when they go after something. But righteous men use their strength to attain riches and do not hurt people during their quest.

The inner strength of a man is put there by God as part of the core of his mental state. God made man and woman differently not only physically but emotionally as well.   It's time to embrace the way we were designed instead of attempting to make ourselves manlier if you are a woman or more feminine if you are a man. To run from the way you were designed is open rebellion against your creator. That is a battle you will lose. It is impossible to rid yourself of the gender "programming" that was placed into you by God. It's a program that can't be fully wiped out of your system.

No matter how hard you try.

So, women, go after the things in this life that you want to obtain and do it the way a virtuous woman would do it, with grace and class.

And men, go after the things in this life that you want to obtain and do it the way a righteous man would do it, with the strength of your hands and the sweat of your brow.

So simply put this Proverb is a contrast of the different ways righteous men and women go about achieving goals.

Women attain things by graciousness and men by strength.

Neither is seen as being preferable over the other.

11:17

Ahab was once the king of Northern Israel in the Old Testament. He married a woman named Jezebel and together they ruled with a level of cruelty that superseded what any evil king before them had ever done. They troubled Israel for 22 years. If it was evil or ungodly they would do it and support it. They never once considered that the hardships they experienced during their reign were the result of the choices they had made. In fact Ahab blamed all their troubles on a prophet of God named Elijah.

"When Ahab saw Elijah, Ahab said to him, "Is it you, you troubler of Israel?"" 1 Kings 18:17 (ESV)

Because "of course" it's always the "pastor's fault" for the "trouble" someone is experiencing.

Elijah knew that wasn't true, so he responded…

"…I have not troubled Israel, but you have, and your father's house, because you have abandoned the commandments of the Lord…" 1 Kings 18:18b (ESV)

In short, Elijah was saying "I didn't do this to you, you did this to yourself."

There are people in this life that you and I will encounter that intend to not only do us harm but bring harm upon others because of the cruel manner in which they choose to live. With each cruel act they instigate against someone else (whether in an organization or to an individual) they wind up not only harming their target but also themselves. The crazy thing is that when they reap the trouble that was caused by their actions they tend to blame that trouble on someone else. After all, it can't be their fault; it has to be someone else's. So their target becomes the friend, family member, or religious leader that pointed out their wrong doing. Yet even when they blame someone else for their hurt, they can't escape this fact…

"…a cruel man hurts himself." Proverbs 11:17 (ESV)

Joseph is a man that is spoken of in Genesis that grew up under some unfortunate circumstances. His brothers hated him and sold him into slavery which separated him from his home and all that was familiar. As a slave he gained respect and was given a high position in his master's house. This was a position that few slaves were ever able to achieve. This all ended one day when his master's wife told a lie about him. That lie not only landed him in prison but also placed the blame of her sin on him. While in prison, he gained the highest position a prisoner could hold, which placed him into a situation where he was able to interpret dreams for two "royal" prisoners who promised to tell Pharaoh about him after they were released. It took two years for his name to be brought to the attention of Pharaoh and he was released from prison. Once he was freed, he was exalted to being the second in command over the whole land of Egypt. Never once did he treat anyone in his life cruelly. In fact when he was reunited with his brothers he treated them with mercy; mercy that he displayed in all his relationships. He was kind to people, even the ones who meant him harm. In doing this he reaped the good that came from a life lived with kindness and mercy. Because…

"*When you're kind to others, you help yourself; when you're cruel to others, you hurt yourself.*" Proverbs 11:17 (MSG)

We will never (more than likely) be in a position like Ahab, who was King of Israel, or like Joseph, who was second in command over an entire nation, or like the prophet Elijah, for that matter. But we do have a choice, just like they did, to place ourselves in a position to either be blessed because of our choices or to be hurt by them. If we choose to treat people with kindness and mercy in this life, good will come our way. If we choose to be cruel towards others, it will bring ourselves much harm.

When I was young, there was this neighborhood kid that began to come to our church. He wasn't nice and picked on several kids at the church including me. He was always trying to instigate a fight or a negative reaction from us. In most instances, he was successful. We didn't like him and there were many reasons why.

So we created the A-Team, a group of kids whose first mission was to get even with this bully. We wrote not-so-nice letters, clipped them to his mail box, rang his door bell and ran for cover; knowing he would be the one to answer the door and receive the cards firsthand. We watched from our hiding spot each time he collected them from the mailbox. This worked well for a while and our cruelty seemed to be winning the day, until his Grandma showed up in church one Sunday morning with all those cards we had written in tow.

It wasn't one of my finer moments and brought me much harm. In fact, from that day on, it hindered the relationships I had with those friends that joined my quest. Not only did we get in trouble with our parents, it hurt our interactions with each other.

"...when you are cruel to others you hurt yourself." Proverbs 11:17 (MSG)

We all have people in our lives that are "living issues." They do not treat us right when we are around and have done things to hurt us in this life. Our natural response to people like that is to bring them harm, to be as cruel to them as they were to us. If we decide to meet their cruelty with some cruel acts of our own it becomes a no win situation and we wind up multiplying our own hurt.

No one has ever been blessed from a cruel act.

But plenty of people have been blessed by living a life of kindness and mercy.

You and I have the power to determine if the future will bring us blessings or hurt.

Joseph was the master of mercy and kindness. Even when he was testing the loyalty and truthfulness of his brothers he was still being kind and merciful to them. He was careful, and didn't allow them to get but so close to him. This means that kindness and mercy isn't a doorway of instance acceptance. There are people in this life we must not allow back into our lives at the level of involvement they once had. We may have to set boundaries; but when we do, it can't be because we are somehow lashing out at those people. Even after those boundaries are established, we still must treat those people with kindness and mercy, though they do not deserve it.

Remember, you and I either put into motion future moments of regret, hardship and judgment by choosing to be cruel or future moments of blessing and peace when we choose to be kind and merciful. The results of those choices, good or ill are never "Elijah's fault"...

they are ours, and ours alone.

"When you're kind to others, you help yourself; when you're cruel to others, you hurt yourself." Proverbs 11:17 (MSG)

11:18

I have been looking for a used vehicle lately and have had conversations with many salesmen (no ladies yet) about certain vehicles of interest to me. In these situations I am never really sure how honest they are being about the car they are trying to sell. Sometimes what they are saying does not match the car I'm looking at, nor the quality of the rest of vehicles on their lot.

Sometimes salesmen "overstate things."

And that's a nice way of putting it.

Just the other day I was at a car lot and a salesman was talking with me about a car I was interested in, as if it was not only "the best car he had ever had" on his lot but it might have been the best car that he had ever had the privilege to sell. Now, he didn't say those words exactly, but the way he presented the car made me feel like I would be a fool to pass up buying a car like that one. The problem was the car was a piece of junk, just like every other car on his lot and it was way overpriced.

But, I understand what he was doing. If you are trying to sell a high priced piece of junk to someone you have to exaggerate its value to the customer so you can convince them to purchase. If you don't they will move on to something else.

You have to make the car look more valuable than it really is.

In fact, at one point in our conversation he said it was a very "rare" car. This was a funny statement because he had 3 more just like it (two were a different color so maybe we will give him that) same model and make on his lot.

This was deception at its best.

He really should have taken up politics.

"The wicked earns deceptive wages..." Proverbs 11:18a

A few years ago I was in need of a vehicle for myself. My Audi had been totaled by a deer.

My first 8 pointer.

After searching and searching for a vehicle that was in my price range, I finally found one on a friend's lot and bought the car from him. He told me everything that had ever been done to the car (as far as he knew) including the fact that he had the transmission rebuilt. 100,000 miles later I am still completely satisfied with the vehicle and would buy from him again. The only reason I haven't currently is because he doesn't have a vehicle I'm interested in on his lot.

But he isn't just honest with people he knows…

he deals with every customer the same way, regardless if he knows them or not. He will not sell a car that he is not comfortable with driving himself. It is a righteous value that drives him and his business. He is truthful with people and people can be truthful with him. Because of this, his car lot is known in the community for having good cars and he is known for the honest way he runs his business.

"*but one who sows righteousness gets a sure reward.*" Proverbs 11:18b

A very "raw" translation of this verse would be… "*… but one who sows righteousness his reward shall be truth.*" (PBP)

Truth

This not only goes for car dealers and their businesses, it goes for whatever you are involved with that makes you money. If you mow yards, have a handyman business, own a barber shop, groom dogs, paint for a living, or sell insurance, etc… Honesty is always the best business policy. If you are honest you will reap the benefits and blessings of being honest. Not only will others be honest and fair with you but your reputation will be trustworthy and respectable.

That's a "true" reward.

Yes, there will be those who are dishonest with you from time to time, that is just the way of life, but those types of people will be few and far between. The path of honest business practices enables you to learn quickly who you should do business with and who you shouldn't. Honesty will enable you to put your head on your pillow at night knowing that God approves of your business practices and is happy with you.

That reward alone is worth it all.

People who are honest in their business dealings bring God much joy.

He delights in them

Remember – "*A false balance is an abomination to the Lord, but a just weight is his delight.*" Proverbs 11:1 (ESV)

It is hard though to stay righteous in your business dealings. It seems that those who deceive and push their way to the top, never being truthful with anyone, 'succeed' in this life. But what are they really achieving? The very deception that is used for their seemingly successful life poisons every wage they earn and every relationship they build. Furthermore, they are always suspicious of people they are dealing with because deep down they know, because of the deceptive way they do business, they are also doing business with other deceptive people. People who may not be telling them the truth. People who can't be trusted.

That's a bad way to make money…

but that is the quality of wage that has been earned. They never really feel good and proud about what they have accomplished. The fact that God hates their false business practices sends them to bed each night knowing God isn't pleased with what they are doing…

and that's a wage that isn't worth having.

"*Bad work gets paid with a bad check; good work gets solid pay.*" Proverbs 11:18 (MSG)

11:19

It's a matter of life and death

you choose

Those who choose to be steadfast in righteousness obtain life

but if you take the unrighteous path "warning"

it's a dead end road….

literally.

Each day we live, we reach out to something, things that are either evil or righteous.

What are you inclined to reach out for? Is your heart at a state in which by default it reaches out to righteousness? Do you follow God in such a way or have you made the "right decisions" (according to Scripture) in your lifetime that now just by habit you will choose the right way? Have you submitted to God in such a way that He has created in you a clean heart and it has grown to where it is genuine in all the things it reaches for?

It is a heart that has been changed by God that reaches out to righteousness as a guide for its life…. and the end result is that is what it obtains. Life

Genuine life.

What are you inclined to reach out for? Is your heart still in the state you were born with? Do you pursue things you were told were evil but you continue reaching out for them? Because for you, you do not see the big deal because you get a certain level of fulfillment from those things you reach out for and do on a daily or weekend basis…

or is it that you just really don't believe there is a right way at all. All that really matters is what is right for you. So you continue to reach out for those types of things… not realizing how evil those things really are and even though you are feeling good and great, those things are really leading to death

You know that the Bible says they're not right but you reach out for them anyway…

Maybe, it's time to make a change and reach for something else that doesn't lead to death.

Reach out to Jesus and the way he describes for us to live this life.

Warning – results along the way may vary but will all end with life

and that's a lot better than death.

11:20

What is going on in your heart? That is what really matters.

"Those of crooked heart are an abomination to the Lord, but those of blameless ways are his delight." Proverbs 11:20 (ESV)

The word crooked describes one who is twisted and crooked at his very core…

twisted and crooked in his heart…

her mind – twisted

his emotions – crooked

his will – perverse

twisted, perverse, and crooked, turned in every direction except in the direction of righteousness

So twisted they think that their lifestyle is ok.

It's the people that take pictures of odd sorts of stuff.   Trying to show they are cool, ok and living a great life they take pictures of weird items like…

beer bottles

I'm not saying the Bible says drinking is wrong… it says getting drunk is wrong and it also warns of the influence that strong drink can have on you. The Bible teaches that extreme caution must be taken if you partake… but that is a can of worms for another time.

I am saying there is something twisted about taking a picture of your beer bottle like you would take a picture of your child or a sunset and then posting it for all to see…

It's a beer bottle not a car.

It's the spouse who all of a sudden says one day "I'm no longer in love with you" and leaves.

What does that mean "no longer in love"? How is that possible? Doesn't the Bible teach that love never fails?

There's something twisted about that statement… and crooked. For it does nothing but hurt the people around them… including the little ones "they created"…

but it even goes one step further when they think "the kids will be alright"….

yes, they will survive and adjust, but things will never be as good as they could have been, and for the rest of their lives they will deal with the decision that has just been made…

its twisted…. and crooked.

Now I'm not saying that every divorced person is doomed to hell…

I think that's unfair.

Nor am I saying that everyone that gets a divorce is twisted and crooked…

nope… for I know people (trust me) who… with what the spouse did came out of nowhere… one day they woke up and found they had been cheating on them or they woke up to the "I don't love you anymore", or they had endured beatings long enough (and twisted would be enduring more than once).

What I am saying is, if we believe for a moment that things will be much better and no one will feel the effects of what we are doing or are about to do, that sort of thinking is twisted. Every divorce, no matter the reason, leaves a wake of scars for people to deal with and be reminded of the rest of their days.

No matter the reason.

It's the constant sitting down in front of the computer and looking at pornography and convincing yourself this is ok. That your spouse's non-interest in sex has driven you to this and it's ok for you to have to have some sort of release. It's the twisted thinking that says God is fine with it all, and you can just repent and go on. So, you do, you repent and go on, but find yourself in the exact same spot time and time again. Looking then confessing until looking and confessing becomes your twisted crooked way of life. And even though the confessions make it seem that you are trying to follow God, the constant going back reveals your rebellious heart, your twistedness that is inside.

"It was ok for me to lie about that"

"It was OK for me to hit them"

"It was ok for me to lose my temper and yell at them, I was justified in doing so"

"It was OK for me to kill them"

"I was just driving the car"

"I was just in the wrong place at the wrong time"

"Christians are stupid"

"Christians hate people"

"I do not need religion, I do not need God"

"We should be tolerant of everyone"

All these statements come from a very dark place in a person's heart, a heart that is twisted and crooked.

A heart that is far from God.

Sometimes these people are in the open about it and at other times, they try to cover it up but they do not fool God because he sees their crooked ways… that their hearts are twisted confused, crooked and turned in every direction except in the direction of righteousness…

in every direction except in the direction of God and His ways….

"Those of crooked heart are an abomination to the Lord, but those of blameless ways are his delight." Proverbs 11:20 (ESV)

But those who are blameless, who desire to be so at the very core of their being

their heart desires it

they walk as best they can to follow Him and His ways…

they are without blemish, whole and upright…

their ways are straight and sure, heading in only one direction…

to please God.

Those people are His delight.

His delight.

I want to be His delight. To live my life with a heart that is in tune with pleasing Him.

The blameless are the ones who have cried out to God because they have no other place to go. They realize their heart is desperately wicked and they need guidance on how to live this life better. They are the ones who cry out to God from the very core of their being, desiring a change, desiring His help, wanting His forgiveness and for Him to change their very soul…

for Him to change their core, to keep it straight and untwisted.

Jesus does that for us, through His sacrifice on the cross He provided a sure way to untwist our hearts, a way to live straight and for the Lord.

For all who accept Him and live for Him as a result of that, they become God's delight.

God's Joy.

Jesus is really the only way we can live blamelessly in this life, He is the only one that can straighten our paths and heal our twisted hearts.

I want to be His delight… His Joy…

I do not want to be something He hates…

Blameless is not moral perfection but speaks of the wholeness and integrity of one's heart and behavior.

If that is what you desire pray this prayer…

Lord, I'm sorry for my twisted ways, please forgive me for all the crooked paths I have taken, the sins I have committed, the times I've confessed but went right back to my evil ways… please forgive me for those… I accept Jesus as my Savior today, I want Him to straighten me out and untwist my twistedness. I desire for the Holy Spirit to teach me the truths from Your Word that will guide me and give me principles concerning how to live… for I have lived my way far too long… it's past time for me to turn myself completely over to You… in Jesus' name… Amen

11:21

Are they really going to get away with that… again?

Have you ever thought that?

I have

of course you may have termed it differently, like…

Why do they always succeed when they are doing what they are doing in a multi-evil sort of way? How do these guys, who do not obey the rules, who do things their way, who cut and back stab to make their way to the top, always seem to get the promotions or win the day?

If you are in a moment today or anytime in the future where you think the wicked are winning and will win remember the promise of this verse for today….

"Assuredly the evil man will not go unpunished…."

It will happen; it's just a matter of time.

You may never see it happen, but it will happen, it's just a matter of time.

They may "win this round", "win this day" or gain ground on you but their victory is only temporary and isn't really a victory at all because all they have done is secured their punishment…

their reckoning

for assuredly they will not go unpunished.

For you…

if you are a child of God and are living accordingly…

there is a different fate for you

you are going to be delivered

in fact

you are delivered

it may not feel like it, you may not realize it or know it but God is in the business of saving His people from things.

the promotion you didn't get and the "cut throat" did was a circumstance that took place where God delivered you from something

Yes they may have smeared your name

Yes they may have stepped on your shoulders to get the position

but these things are temporary and will pass

but God just saved you from something more permanent and more far reaching

it could have been a temptation that comes with that position, to work longer hours to sacrifice your family, to be "owned" by the company, enslaved by its practices.

He may have delivered you from having to deal with pressure, and being faced with moral tensions that would come with that position or thing.

You have been delivered.

If it is oppression, you feel that the big man is putting you down and you think they are winning at suppressing your beliefs. I'm not saying it isn't serious, nor am I saying that it doesn't hurt and cause a certain level of fear which leads to you feeling defeated because it looks like they're winning….

I'm just saying

because this proverb is saying

that you are headed toward deliverance and they are headed for punishment for God will not allow their wrong doing to go unanswered (even though He will take His time in administering justice) and He will deliver you from the things that would really harm your life…

for you have the victory through Him over your opponent

who is really an opponent of Christ

and judgment for that opponent belongs to Christ alone

and He will administer it in His timing…

So be encouraged.

11:22

I can't help it…

I cannot get the image of a pig with a nose ring out of my mind.

Can't you see it?

A pig with a snout piercing?

"Ham Hawing" around

Eating anything and everything you throw into the trough.

Yep… good ol' slop – the pig doesn't know or care to discern what it is eating…

to the pig it all goes to the same place…

and food gets caught in the nose ring and drips down into the pig's mouth…

and the pig doesn't care.

You never see a pig running through a field, achieving goals, working, or doing anything productive. You never see a pig making any type of beneficial decision, or giving any consideration on how it is living its life and how it is affecting others.

Nope…

The sausage you ate for breakfast this morning once lived a life of eating, grunting, sleeping, rolling (in mud), and napping.

The bacon you ate once lived a life with no discretion… it just did whatever it felt like doing at the moment and never achieved anything in life…

And do you know who the proverb says is like a pig with a nose ring?

"…A beautiful woman who doesn't have discretion." Proverbs 11:22

A woman who lives her life not caring about making the right sort of choices. A woman that is beautiful but lives her life with the discretion of a pig.

She's Beautiful but she says whatever she wants, when she wants to say it and doesn't consider the hurtfulness of her words.

She's Beautiful but she wears whatever she wants, as low or high as she wants. Not caring about the uncomfortable effect it has on others, friends or otherwise.

She's Beautiful but spends money without thinking and runs up credit card debt and never considers the stress and bondage her actions cause. In fact… like a pig she just doesn't care.

She's beautiful but doesn't really care for her children. She uses them as trophies, items she can show off to get attention (and sympathy) and then gets irritated with the responsibility they bring.

She's beautiful but her beauty is like a gold ring…

and that gold ring is really attached to the snout of a pig…

the only beauty a pig's nose gets.

Her life is without discretion…

like a pig's…

and it's worthless.

But "*a gracious woman gets honor*" (11:16) She lives her life with discretion, grace and care. She follows the paths of righteousness with her lips and actions. She adds value to those around her and she accomplishes many things.

She refuses to live the life of a pig.

Therefore she is a woman of honor… one you would want to know.

11:23

There is only one way this can turn out

Only one way

and in many respects the way it turns out

the way anything turns out

is predetermined

but not by God

by us

Way before we do anything, participate in any event or action, the driving force behind all we do is in motion, propelling us to whatever end our heart has set our course toward.

The condition of your heart determines the condition of your end.

If your heart is good, all you set out to do ends up being…

good.

If your heart is wicked, all you set out to do ends up being…

bad.

If your heart is wicked and you look like you have a good heart, all you set out to do ends up being…

bad.

If your heart is good and people think you are wicked, all you set out to do ends up being…

good.

The expectation of your heart sets you on a path headed for good or ill.

Of course the path, while on it, doesn't always look or feel like the place it is headed. The heart that desires to follow God, more often than not, looks more evil than good. Trials and tests of faith spring up along the way making the path bumpy. Storms arise, burdens are placed on your shoulders to bear along the way and the "nature" of all the bad things that occur can bring someone to the point where they may rethink their choice and desire to follow God.

Have you ever had that happen? You have striven to follow God to the best of your ability. You allowed him to mold and change your heart but then times become so dire you wondered if you placed your faith in the wrong place. You wondered how things could be so bad when all you desire is to do well, for God's glory.

Sometimes the way the path looks and feels isn't indicative of how it will end.

For the heart that is wicked, that rejects all God says in the Bible (or even part of it) concerning good and evil, more often than not, that path looks like the preferable path to be on. Things seem to go well on the surface of that path. Yes, there are some inward troubles but they are easily ignored or covered up by the picture that is painted in one's mind, a picture that lies about how well things are going. A lie that is believed but never fully. If a trial does become public on this path an evil heart just weasels its way out of it, it is never their fault, always someone else's. The best deception is a redirecting focus onto others. A strategy that seems to work very well…

until the end.

Sometimes the way the path looks and feels isn't indicative of how it will end.

"The desire of the righteous ends only in good; the expectation of the wicked in wrath."
Proverbs 11:23 (ESV)

But what about Christians? Their intents are always good right?

Nope…

Sometimes Christians are just Christians in name only. Just saying you are one doesn't determine your end nor does it mean your heart is truly changed. There are a lot of Christians who live wickedly and seem to be getting away with it.

But

Sometimes Christians are Christians because Jesus has redeemed their hearts. They follow the ways of God even when they do not understand them, even when it hurts to do so. They are constantly submitting their heart's desires and adopting God's. To be on the right path takes a certain mindset that comes from a changed heart. A heart that is changed by Jesus.

Sometimes a Christian's heart is flavored with good desires and other times it has wicked intentions. Proverbs 11:23 not only speaks of a lifelong pattern of events that leads to a certain type of end but also short things we become involved with. Those desires also end in the same manner by which they were birthed. If they were conceived by an evil heart they will not end well; but if they have their roots in a righteous heart, things will end well. Sometimes good Christians set an event in motion they regret and find themselves asking God's forgiveness for being involved. Forgiveness, though it doesn't prevent the end from happening, does open a door for the heart to be motivated in the future differently because of God's work to change it.

How is your heart today? What Motivates you?

Wickedness or Good?

A quick look at how things end in your life (short term or long term) will reveal what the answer of those two questions really should be.

11:24

Recently, I took on the project of cleaning out our attic. We had stuff stored up there that had not been used in over 7 years. The goal of the project: to get rid of all the stuff that we never use or think about to make room to store the things we use from time to time, like Christmas Decorations. Over the past few months we have given away a bunch of stuff, clothes, kitchen items, etc… they are now in homes where people are using them. There was also a lot of stuff that had to be thrown away. It seems being stored in the attic for so long of a time had taken its toll.

In the end, whether given away or thrown in the trash, we didn't need all that stuff, we were just holding on to it; just to hold on to it.

Weird.

That's the way it is for most of us I would imagine. We have stuff that we hold onto just in case we might need it one day. Some of us hold on to money, others of us hold on to things we have acquired, storing them because one day we "might need them." Most people are not givers by nature, most people love to receive (this includes the people you know who say they enjoy seeing people open gifts they have given to them).

Human nature is inclined to hold on tightly to what is "ours". It brings us a sense of security to know we still have some stuff we might need.

Human nature usually holds even tighter to money and seldom gives that away.

The natural tendency is to think that if I hold on to what I have, I will have more because it's there now and I will add to it later. If I give it away I might not have what I need when I need it. After all, that bill is coming due or, "you never know what might happen and we need to be prepared."

"One gives freely, yet grows all the richer; another withholds what he should give, and only suffers want." Proverbs 11:24 (ESV)

This verse teaches that the more we hold onto possessions the less we will have, but the more we give away the more we will have. I don't know if you took math in school but that's not how we have been trained to think, mathematically. Subtraction means you no longer have the amount you subtracted…

end of story.

But in life, though it doesn't work in a mathematics course, it's the people who let go and give that wind up having more than the people who are stingy.

This is really a hard lesson for me because I am somewhat stingy at times, but I know people who seem to have no trouble giving stuff away.

A friend of mine owns his own lawn company and sometimes mows people's lawns for free. He has never lost money when doing this.

I know that sounds crazy, but it's true.

A friend of mine gave me an iMac back in 2006. I was tickled. At the time I didn't know him that well, but he befriended me and the ministry at the church where I was serving. That computer is still running strong today… it was a blessing.

Another friend, who during a time where my lawn mower was "down for the count," gave me one of his. I've tried to return it several times but he doesn't want it back. Recently, we gave that mower to another family to use. It's still going strong.

Another set of friends (because they are married) continually give things away. It is not abnormal to catch them in a grocery store buying groceries for a family in need or a family who has had a loved one in the hospital for so long they have not had time to go grocery shopping so they do it for them and give them the groceries free of charge. I have seen them pay for vacations for other people and even help out families with some bills when times were tough. They have never been lacking though they give a lot of what they earn away.

I met another friend in a parking lot last night who gave us tickets to the next Wake Forest vs Carolina Basketball game. He also has never been lacking, nor his parents who have always had the same giving attitude.

In fact, none of these friends of mine have ever seemed to be lacking. These are people who are blessed, not just with money but with strong relationships. The person who waits until they have enough money so they can give will end up never having enough money or strong relationships. If you have to have enough to hold on to before you can let go, that's not giving and you will never give to anyone. You will never bless someone with what you have, that you could have given, with no thought of payment in return.

"The world of the generous gets larger and larger; the world of the stingy gets smaller and smaller." Proverbs 11:24 (MSG)

As counterintuitive as this verse sounds, it is true. Those who give to others increase and those who hold tightly to what they have acquired decrease into a mental state of just wanting more.

Maybe it's time to "scatter" some things you have and quit worrying about losing those items (or that money). Remember the more we give the more we increase and the more we tighten our grip on what we have the more we lose.

Lord, help me to be a person that gives.

11:25

Fat

that is what this verse is about

Being Fat

in fact the first line of this verse could read

"The soul of blessing will be made fat"

In the day this was written, and even in our day (if you consider the world and not just America's perspective); If you were fat, you were rich and blessed….

Here it is saying that the one who gives to others, the one who blesses others, will be enriched.

We live in a society that is careful giving to others. We have stuff, keep more stuff, hoard stuff and never give stuff away. Because, to have it, is more of a value to us than blessing someone by giving them things that we have that they need.

Here, the more we give to others… bless others; the more our lives are enriched.

This is not just speaking of money; money is really a small part of what is being talked about here. There are other gifts we can give people….

other blessings we can share.

Like a smile

as simple as that sounds you would be surprised at how much people need to see a smile. A smile communicates they're worth something, you are glad to see them or they'll be ok stick with it, or I like you. Messages that many in this world need.

And the more you smile the more people smile back at you. The more people become glad to see you.

"Whoever" or the "soul" represents a person's inner drive that is expressed in their actions. The blessings that are given are the result of a soul that is strong enough to give them, a soul that is changed or impacted by God's grace enough to share. A soul that isn't selfish but has others as its focus.

It's when a person cannot help but bless others....

and here, it seems, we are all capable of this type of care. We can all bless the people around us and the return for doing that is far more "fattening" than we think is possible and is more fulfilling than if we only bless ourselves.

It comes down to your water....

the phrase "he who waters will be watered" is the same sort of phrase as "what you sow you shall also reap." If someone waters someone else then they too will get water in return.

But not all water is good water.

Water can be refreshing and up lifting to our spirits. On a day that is hot a sprinkle of cool water is just what is needed. It makes us feel good... blessed if you will.

When we water people with love, mercy, peace, and forgiveness we will also be watered with that same sort of thing.

But if the day was cold and someone sprayed us with water... well that's a different situation all together. A moment where we would feel anything but blessed.

If we water people, soak them down with anger, hate, or any other negative emotion we will be watered with the same thing....

Let's say you have a friend named Bob who did something bad toward you and you just can't bring yourself to forgive him. He hurt you, what he did against you was just wrong and bad. You can't give him forgiveness because he needs to pay. So, you are making him pay for what he has done to you with all your capabilities.

3 months down the road when you do something wrong (which is something we all fall into from time to time), what do you think you will be watered with?

right….

and even though you will now desire to receive forgiveness as Bob once did, You will not receive it…. because you will get what you watered with a few months ago.

Of course had you watered differently, with love, mercy, forgiveness…. then what you received during your fall would be the very thing you desired.

What if the water we extend to others was refreshing and not fueled by our irritations or anger?

Would that change our relationships?

Would it enrich them and us?

Yes, because

"… *whoever refreshes others will be refreshed.*" Proverbs 11:25b (NIV)

11:26

Let's wait until the price skyrockets then we will sell what we have

We know there is a need

We know there is a famine

We know there are people in want

But that doesn't matter for we need to make more

money

So right now things are not for sale that people need, we will sell them at the opportune moment when it's financially beneficial for us

for that's what matters

This is what is called being a profiteer instead of a neighbor.

Those that choose to live this way are cursed, not highly thought of, in their communities. Because what is being withheld is a need of the people, a need that determines whether or not a family will survive. And when someone has something they could sell to people who really need it and their reason for not selling is for profit reasons, people do not take that very well, for it is cruel.

After all the people are not asking for it for free, they are not asking for a hand out, they do not want welfare…

they just want to buy a share of food

just enough to keep going another day.

The word here for withhold represents something that is withheld that only God or his appointed authorities have the power to withhold. In this context it is when someone withholds something that causes injury to another.

And when you are withholding something from those in need, you are playing God and causing needless injuries to those around you.

But the one who sells during the time of need is blessed.

Interesting that it is not blessings on him who gives without selling what he has. Instead the blessing is on the head of the one who sells people the things they need so they can survive. They are looked at by their communities with honor, with a sense of thankfulness. For these people have their neighbors' good will as their motivation instead of how to make more money.

It is Joseph in Egypt; who stored grain for 7 years and sold it when the entire world faced a terrible famine. He sold it to all who came for it. Being placed there by God, he withheld during the years of plenty and sold during the years of famine.

The result was people survived, not only Egyptians, but the whole world (as they knew it at the time) as well, including his family.

And he was blessed, honored, thought well of. Because his goal wasn't to make a profit, it was to serve God in the position he had been given.

We Americans generally have a lot of stuff. And sometimes there are family members and friends who need things. Are we willing to sell them what we have at a fair price so they can survive?

Yes it is good to give things to people; I think we have established that fact in the previous chapters…

but it is also good to sell things as well.

It gives us a fair price for the things we have in abundance, and it allows the ones who are buying from us to maintain a certain level of dignity.

So if you have it…. sell it if someone needs it

Do not hold onto it for profit's sake….

"People curse the one who hoards grain, but they pray God's blessing on the one who is willing to sell." Proverbs 11:26 (NIV)

11:27

What is your number one focus for today?

Is it to invest and give to your community?

Is your number one priority today to figure out how you can contribute to your workplace and make its environment better?

Is your goal to treat those around you with love and kindness?

or

Is your number one focus today to get back at those who have hurt you?

To do what it takes to succeed even if it means stepping on people to get there?

Is your number one goal today to make your spouse or children know how disappointed you are in them and punish them anyway you can?

Is your number one goal to stir something up with the people you interact with or is it your priority to bring hope and to bless those you come in contact with?

These are the questions this verse demands us to ask ourselves, for I am sure that you would rather have "favor" coming your way in your community rather than adversity.

"Whoever" this means all of us can choose this if we desire it.

"Whoever diligently seeks"; diligently comes from a word that means to look early, like first thing in the morning…

you know the early bird and the worm.

Here it denotes a priority in looking…

in searching

in seeking…

"Whoever diligently seeks good…"

Whoever seeks good as a top priority for any day they live. Those who make doing good, seeking how they can make a positive difference in their communities at their workplace or in their homes…

"…seeks favor" will find favor coming their way.

It is when you and I wake up in the morning and say…

Thank You Lord for this day… what do You want me to do to make it better in my small neck of the woods? Show me where I can make a difference for You.

"Whoever diligently seeks…" Seeks here comes from a word that means one who is striving to do something by any method. "Whoever" makes it their number one priority of everyday they live to seek out ways to make their community better, ways to do good and make a difference…

favor will come to them in return.

It is not that we go out to please other people so they will please us.

No

It's that we go out purposing to do good deeds no matter where we go with no thought of getting something in return. We live to Impact our community for good for the Glory of God and His son Jesus and that is enough for us. It is enough just to see the effects in the lives of those around us of the good we have done.

It is when we diligently seek to live Impactful lives that we actually gain favor with those around us… in our communities, at our work place and in our homes.

Will there be those that oppose us?

Yes…

but they will be few

the majority of the people whose lives are impacted by our investment will recognize and appreciate our efforts…

They will like us and favor will come our way.

It would be great if you and I heeded this wisdom. When we put others first and seek their welfare, we are ultimately seeking our own good though that is not our number one objective.

But what if someone searches for something else?

What if they search for evil?

What if our number one priority is to get back at someone?

What if our number one priority is to advance our own agenda?

What if our number one priority is to improve our own lives and if someone else is having a hard time "oh well"? What if we do not really care what happens to them while we are achieving our goals?

What if our number one priority is to make someone pay for how they treated us?

"but evil…" Evil comes from a word that means adversity, unhappiness, or hardships. It's when we create bad situations for other people for our own prideful benefit. It's when we seek to cause injury to someone else, when we focus on hurting the one or ones that have hurt us deeply.

"but evil comes to him who searches for it"

Simply put if we set out as our number one priority to get even by stirring up mischief with someone else….

those chickens will come home to roost at our house.

and just in case you missed the roosting reference…

When we set out to destroy, and cause more pain to happen

we lose

favor passes us by

and the very harm we intended for someone else…

becomes ours to bear.

So

What is your number one focus today?

Is it to change your environment for the better?

Or is it to hurt others so that inevitably you will bear more pain?

"Whoever diligently seeks good seeks favor, but evil comes to him who searches for it."
Proverbs 11:27 (ESV)

11:28

Just the other day a person began to follow me on Twitter. Someone I do not know. I checked out their Twitter page just to see who they were. The first tweet I read of theirs was this one...

"If you are rich that means you have stolen something to get there."

The second one read…

"If you are poor someone has stolen from you."

The third one read…

"The poor never steal from anyone."

So needless to say I didn't begin to follow this individual. I am neither rich (according to USA standards) nor poor. I tug on the bottom end of the middle class. So, believe me when I say this…

It is not a sin to be rich.

Just ask Abraham

Isaac

Jacob

or

Job

These men prove you can follow God by faith, live righteously and be rich at the same time. It seems our culture today is warring against those with money, to their own detriment. It could be said in a parabolic form that…

"The less a rich person makes the less an economy can grow and flourish."

Scripture does not teach that every rich person is evil no more than it teaches that every poor person is lazy and stupid. Righteousness at any economic level is determined by a person's heart. Financial standing does not show how good or bad your heart is. All economic levels have good people in them and bad.

And NO

just to be clear…

one doesn't have more good people in it than the other.

"Trust in your money and down you go! But the godly flourish like leaves in spring." Proverbs 11:28 (NLT)

Here, what a person puts their trust in determines if they fail in the end or succeed.

Everybody has riches. The poor, the middle class and the rich. All people find themselves faced with the choice of putting their faith into the money they have or don't have but want.

For the rich, this choice determines how much they give

For the middle class, it determines how much they give

For the poor, it determines how much they give

Poor people can trust in money just as much as any other social class. The pursuit of money, either through it being given to them as a hand out or earning it while complaining about their employer, is a sign of a heart that trusts in money and not in God. It drives their jealousy of all those who have more than them.

But isn't this true of middle class people as well as the rich?

Yes.

Humans have a tendency to trust in the dollar, for security, and for pride and a sense of accomplishment. When we put our trust in money it brings about "all sorts of evil" and will fail everyone who has made it his pursuit in life.

Like a leaf that falls in the Fall…

if we trust in money it will fail us every time.

But for those who have put their faith in God, they flourish with life.

Like a new leaf that promises life in the spring.

"Whoever trusts in his riches will fall, but the righteous will flourish like a green leaf."
Proverbs 11:28 (ESV)

For the rich, it determines how much they give

For the middle class, it determines how much they give

For the poor, it determines how much they give

Righteous living allows for us to flourish as we live, not because we are becoming rich with money but because we are gaining richness to life. Like a green leaf in the spring, a life of promise, giving to others, helping others, while we follow Christ and put our faith in Him.

Rich or poor

young or old

will have lives that flourish when they walk in righteousness by placing their trust in Jesus…

and Him alone.

11:29

I have seen it and you have too. A person in a family begins to act in ways that seem to rip the fabric of a family unit to pieces. It's the drug addict that mom supports but no one else does. He continues to take advantage of her for his own purposes and the rest of the family is upset about it but seemingly can't do anything to stop it. It's the spouse that chooses to commit adultery or the husband who chooses to not love his wife anymore and they are just waiting for time to pass before the inevitable happens. It's when a person in a family begins to live for herself rather than for the family unit and causes trouble as a result, trouble that never would have happened if she had not become so selfish.

Can we count the ways that a person can trouble his own household? Or can we list the ways we have seen people cause trouble for their families?

Maybe not…

Definitely not here…

but what we can "take to the bank is" the fact that the one who stirs up the trouble gets something as a result of his choices.

Wind

and nothing more.

Grasping for "having it their way", they destroy the substance of what they had with all the trouble they have caused. For all the energy spent on their shallow victories, they wind up with nothing to grasp at all…

except

wind.

It's the drama queen that trumps up situations because she has never been taught or maybe she never cared about, controlling her "out of control feelings." She wants her way, will do anything to be in control and she doesn't trust anyone. If something comes up she makes it more than it really is and will not listen to anyone who tries to bring her back to reality. She is a master of spinning things to her favor, makes herself the victim in every conflict and every situation.

By the time she is through no one remembers what the issue was at first, she has "won" because not only has she covered up the issue, but she has made the person that confronted her to be the bad guy. Thinking she has many friends supporting her and her story, she has destroyed other relationships in the process and has weakened the family unit she still thinks is strong and great. She has grabbed hold of something but it's not what she thinks it is…

it's just wind…

storm winds blow in the direction of her choice. Destroying all who oppose…

destroying her self-esteem and all she holds dear, though she does not realize that is what has happened until it's too late..

As the wind blows through her fingers she is left with…

nothing

"Those who bring trouble on their families inherit the wind…" Proverbs 11:29a (NLT)

It's the man who can't control his temper and constantly attacks his wife and children. Trying to control every aspect of their lives, he gets quite the adrenaline rush…

it feels so good…

but he has destroyed all he sought to control and soon arrives in a position where the only thing he has is

wind

Wind he has blown and wind that remains after he loses his family and the love that could have been. He deeply hurt his wife and has made her scared to be around him. The children are upset not only because of the way he has treated them but because of the way he has treated their mother. As the children grow older they find themselves in marriages and relationships where they do the same thing. Few break free of this and the unhealthy cycle becomes a legacy of wind…

He leaves this world with a legacy of wind and nothing more…

"*Exploit or abuse your family, and end up with a fistful of air; common sense tells you it's a stupid way to live.*" Proverbs 11:29 (MSG)

It's the woman who worries over her children and her husband. She worries about this and she worries about that. Always talking about the next thing she is concerned about, voicing her concern with all the appropriate emotions in tow. This brings a level of stress to her entire family. Stress they would not have if she would be less foolish. All the energy that is spent by her and her family on these emotional roller coasters amounts to nothing more than another emotional ride of hell. Damaged day after damaged day ends with wind being achieved.

Wind she has blown and is now the only thing she and her family are left with.

It's the teenager who decides that Mom and Dad know nothing. Rejecting years of their parents' instruction they live their life, their way. After all they do not understand what the big deal is with all these rules and principles that their parents hold dear.

So, at every turn they find themselves in conflict with the very people who are on their side in this life… their parents. Each action of rebellion cases deep pain to the parents, things are tense in the home, the parents are at a loss as to how to help and fix the issues. The teen thinks it's all the parents fault and they need to change. But this isn't the case. Damaging situation after damaging situation continues to happen, the parents still love their child but are deeply hurt and are at a loss as to what to do.

Soon, many birthdays pass and true maturity finally sets in. The once teenager finds himself/herself looking back on his/her family life and begins to realize how much grief "he" has caused. Then tears come because "she" can see also see where "her" parents were always there for him/her in "his" time of need and the friends that "he" thought were so important fade like the wind…

They had lived foolishly while thinking they were wise and now they see all they had was…

Wind.

The fool never knows what he is losing.

all the drama

all the fights

all the worry

all the resisting…

casts each in the very place he was striving to avoid

with achievements that amount to the worth of…

the wind.

Are you causing any trouble for your family?

The fruit of the trouble you are causing will not be what you think it will be…

It will only be wind.

"Whoever brings ruin on their family will inherit only wind, and the fool will be servant to the wise." Proverbs 11:29 (NIV)

Foolish living never leads to independence.

The drama queen who lives to get her way

The man who controls through anger

The dramatic worrier

or the teenager who knows it all

All want independence from others.

An idea that amounts to wind though the fool may not comprehend that, still finds "himself" serving the wise. The fool doesn't understand that she is serving the wise because the wise are good at what they do. The fool thinks he is independent and important but no one is independent and no one is that important in the scheme of things. In reality we all have to submit to someone so we can provide food and clothing for ourselves.

The foolish just go about life thinking they are in control of everyone including the wise…

but that's very foolish and very far from the truth.

"*and the fool will be servant to the wise of heart*" Proverbs 11:29b (ESV)

Though they may never realize it…

So…

If you think you serve no one….

Well, I'll just let you figure it out.

11:30

An apple

or a pear

or any type of fruit

falls to the ground if not picked and it sits there wasting away to nothing..

or something

for within it are seeds that when covered by the soil below produces something remarkable…

another tree of the same kind…

it is an amazing thing.

When you and I

I and you

decided to follow Jesus and live in the ways He has showed us to live, the righteous ways, the paths that lead to abundant life and wisdom; we produce fruit. In return, fruit is planted in those around us that produce life in others.

It is an amazing thing to consider that the God of all of creation, the Holy One, uses us to pass on His life, His righteousness to others.   That when we live the way He wants us to live…

the right way

the way of wisdom

heeding wise instruction

It not only impacts the quality of our lives

it impacts others as well.

For trees of life sprout up all around us, seen in the positive outcomes of our relationships, planted and born in the lives of those we hang around and invest in…

We see changes in those we have come to know and have gained influence on.

The term tree of life is used throughout Proverbs with its origins in Genesis and the creation accounts. The tree of life represents life as God intended it to be. The tree of life is what He desires for us to get back to.

For those who believe in Him enough for it to change the way that we speak, think and live is to have a taste of that tree…

and once we taste it and pursue it, it is passed on to those around us that we love and cherish.

And that is what happens when we live wisely...

because He who is wise wins souls…

Wins is another word for influences in a positive way… influence for good… influence to the point where others experience God's life.

Influence is not a dictatorship.

Influence is not a set of rules we impart to people and tell them or command them to live this way or else.

Influence is achieved by living what we say

Influence is from living righteous and thus producing fruit after that kind…

fruit that is respectable

fruit that comes from a desire to please God…

fruit that produces an attraction to where others want to be around us and hang with us because there is something positive and good about how we go about our lives.

They taste our fruit without even knowing it or being commanded to do so

and once they taste the fruit, a tree of life sprouts inside of them…

not because the fruit was produced by us…

It was produced by God through us because we chose to live His ways, walk in His path and think His thoughts.

Yes living this the right way has benefits for the person that has chosen to do so… but the real reason…

the real lasting result of that style of life…

is the change in others that have been influenced by the way the righteous one has chosen to live.

For the tree of life isn't just ours to have…

It's for all who believe.

And that is quite *"the green leaf"* – Proverbs 11:28

11:31

The righteous

which we have mentioned several times in this book and are mentioned as God's way for you and I to live are not beyond sinning

Nowhere in Scripture does it say that those who are righteous are perfect, always make the right decisions or always do the right thing.

except for Jesus but He's a bit different than the rest of us, and that is a topic for another time

Righteous people sin...

they get speeding tickets...

say things they should not say...

watch things they should not watch...

have attitudes that are anything but God-honoring

Pride, jealousy, anger, and hate all creep in from time to time because the righteous are just sinners that have chosen to follow God and His ways. In faith they look to Him for guidance in this life though His Word and prayer. In our day, the righteous are those who have accepted the gift of salvation, the death burial and resurrection of Christ, who have believed that Jesus is the Way, the Truth and the Life. They have accepted Him as their Savior and are now given New Life through His resurrection, the Holy Spirit lives in them and helps them make the right choices in this life....

but sometimes they resist the Holy Spirit

Sometimes righteous people choose the wrong path to go down and they pay for their wrong doings. For God disciplines those who are His, who have chosen to be in His family but are living incorrectly.

Surely there is not a righteous man on earth who does good and never sins.
Ecclesiastes 7:20

That is why many among you are weak and sick, and a number of you have fallen asleep. If we were more discerning with regard to ourselves, we would not come under such judgment. When we are judged in this way by the Lord, we are being disciplined so that we will not be finally condemned with the world. 1 Corinthians 11:30-32

My son, do not despise the LORD's discipline, and do not resent his rebuke, because the LORD disciplines those he loves, as a father the son he delights in. Proverbs 3:11-12

In short the righteous are repaid on the earth for the habitual sins they commit. And the one who punishes them is the Lord.

Why does He do this?

Because He loves His people and if they are going down a wrong path, one that is not good for them (because sin never is good for anyone), He disciplines them in order to turn them back from sin.

There are also unavoidable consequences everyone has to face when they make certain choices. Choices that are sinful. If you lie trust is always lost with those to whom you have lied. And even though forgiveness is freely given, forgiveness does not mean that trust is automatically restored. Where the lie is no longer held against you, because you have lied you have created a void in trust, and until time passes and people see you are trustworthy you will not be trusted as much as you would have been if you had just told the truth all along. The break in trust has to be repaid to reestablish it.

And there are times when the righteous ones will not be truthful and even though they repent and ask forgiveness, on this earth there is a price to pay for that.

But the righteous pay for their sins only here on this earth. In eternity, Jesus has taken care of the sin debt of all who have chosen to believe in and live for Him.

And if the righteous ones, the ones who are attempting to follow God, who have accepted the message of the gospel, have to deal with the results of their sin here on earth - they have to repay their wrongs - what do you think will happen to the people who have rejected God, Jesus and His Word?

I shudder to think about it…

For it is time for judgment to begin with God's household; and if it begins with us, what will the outcome be for those who do not obey the gospel of God? And, *"If it is hard for the righteous to be saved, what will become of the ungodly and the sinner?"* 1 Peter 4:17-18

The ones who live their lives running in every direction, except God's direction, must also pay for their actions here on earth. They are judged now and in eternity. We may not see the demise of their sinful lifestyles because they seem, from the outside looking in, to be winning and doing well…

living the dream

but they are really living a nightmare and don't know it…

or maybe they do.

The destructiveness of relationships, emptiness of their hearts, and constant search to fill the emptiness that exists inside them and their fear of death is often hidden but always there.

Their secret is to try to fit in, to go with the trends or make a statement with their lifestyle. The thrill of the attention is fleeting, and when it passes and the days go on, they are left with souls that are empty…

and a life that passes away before their very eyes…

achievements decay

things wear down

bodies fail…

and even though it seems they have escaped judgment, they haven't…

for if God judges His people and makes them repay their wrongs here on earth…

so will the wicked

the difference is the wicked will pay now and pay later

for when a righteous man dies he goes to heaven and receives rewards

but the wicked go to punishment that is eternal…

for all sin debts have to be paid….

and either we accept Jesus' sin debt for our sins or we don't

That's the choice that determines our eternal destiny.

Scripture Copyright Page

Made in the USA
Columbia, SC
17 July 2017